A YEAR INSIDE

PARLIAMENTARY SKETCHES

CRAIG BROWN

Published in 1989 by
Times Books Limited
16 Golden Square
London W1R 4BN

Typeset by CRB Typesetting Services, Ely, Cambs

Printed in Great Britain by
Butler & Tanner Limited
Frome & London

British Library Cataloguing in Publication Data

Brown, Craig
  A year inside
  I. Title
  828'.91409

ISBN 0 7230 03106

FOR FRANCES

CONTENTS

Foreword

A MONTH or so before the start of the 1987 General Election, Frank Johnson rang me up to ask me whether I would like to take over his job as *The Times's* Parliamentary Sketchwriter for a few weeks. He had read a parody of *The Spectator* I had written for *The Tatler*, and he felt that sketchwriting would suit a parodist. This seemed to me rather thin evidence upon which to appoint your successor, but I kept my mouth shut.

My previous experience of Parliament was tiny. The first time I visited the House of Commons was in 1974, to interview Jeremy Thorpe, then Leader of the Liberal Party, for my school magazine. The next time was as a drama student in 1977, to interview John Stonehouse for a play I was writing about him. I remember little about Mr Thorpe, but the memory of Mr Stonehouse hovered in the back of my mind throughout my time as a sketchwriter. I had met him when he was about to face trial but was still a sitting MP. As we walked along the corridors of Westminster together, Mr Stonehouse would greet each passing colleague with an ostentatious "Hello" or "How are you?", and each passing colleague would look the other way, say nothing and bustle onwards. It was like walking with a noisy, gregarious ghost, whom only I could see or hear. I didn't return to Westminster until I became a sketchwriter ten years later, but this remains my strongest impression of MPs: ghostly figures, waving their arms and raising points in an endless bid to see themselves as real and wanted. And parliamentary journalists are riders on the ghost train, occasionally enervated or amused to be brushed by these spooky apparitions, but grateful, nonetheless, to return to the fresh air after their daily spin.

One of the particular privileges of the sketchwriter is that – except during election walkabouts – he has no need to meet politicians face to face. Some sketchwriters voluntarily forego this privilege, hobnobbing with Members over lunch, but I could never see the point. My sketches were singularly bereft of insight into the real person behind the public persona, informed discussion about the development of future policy and up-to-the-minute information about Ministerial rivalries. I treated Parliament as a purely theatrical event, concentrating on the amusement that could be extracted from observing these actors as they dressed as hobgoblins, statesmen or jesters. Very occasionally, I would let an opinion or an almost-serious observation intrude on the Sketch, but I would always regret it. I realise that this was an irresponsible way to treat the seat of democracy, but there seemed to be a sufficient number of responsible people reporting on Parliament to allow for the cackles of at least one mocking bird.

My working day was short, but quite intense. I would clock in at 2.30 in the afternoon, when the first questions are asked in the Chamber. When I first started sketchwriting, I was amazed and terrified by the way in which the subject under discussion changed from minute to minute. Just when you thought you could write a sketch about, say, questions on the Channel Tunnel, the House would suddenly switch to discussing the poor quality of B-roads in the North-East. To write a coherent sketch about something so fidgety and haphazard requires extreme simplification, even from the most conscientious reporters. I tend to think that my best sketches are those which entirely ignore 99% of the goings-on, and concentrate instead on a single harumph from a disgruntled backbencher, or the dress-sense of a senior minister.

After watching the show for an hour and a half or so, I would go for a cup of coffee and a Penguin biscuit to the Press canteen, usually accompanied by my fellow sketchwriters Andrew Rawnsley of *The Guardian* and Mark Lawson of *The Independent*. The generation of sketchwriters which preceded ours seemed to have a reputation of personal antipathy, even stretching to the point of occasional fisticuffs, but the three of us got on very well, and I very much enjoyed our little coffee-breaks. I think that some of the other political journalists, seeing us huddled together, began to suspect that we wrote each other's sketches, but I never really thought about what I was going to write until I had finished the first sentence.

At 4.30, I would shuffle down to *The Times* room, which is conveniently situated only a few yards from the Chamber, and start to write the day's piece on a word-processor. Before Christmas 1987, my deadline was 6.30, but afterwards, thanks to the advances in new technology, it was brought forward to 6.00. Previously, most of my work had come from monthly magazines, where a deadline of six weeks is considered pretty severe, and so the daily prospect of 700 words in a couple of hours at first filled me with dread, particularly as the only politicians I could put a name to were Mr Kinnock, Mrs Thatcher and, on a good day, one or two others. But by the end I came to enjoy this pressure, even setting myself new deadlines to keep my interest up. Quite a few of the later sketches were written in under an hour.

There were many people who made my time as a sketchwriter a happy one. The Political and Parliamentary staff of *The Times* were exceptionally generous with their time and information. Battling against their own deadlines, they were always ready to help me in my struggle for a metaphor, answering questions like "Who was that skinny one in the early Carry On films?" or "Does anyone know the individual names of The Woodentops?" while they should have been getting on with their reports on budget deficits and so on. I would like to thank them all, and in particular Ivan Barnes, whose endless top-notch jokes never succeeded in concealing his great kindness.

One of the joys of the job was the companionship of the man who, the day after Mrs Thatcher's speech to the Conservative Party conference, became my father-in-law. Right from the beginning, Colin Welch gave me much help and encouragement, and his impersonations of many of our leading politicians make me chuckle just to think of them.

I want to thank Frank Johnson for offering me the job, and Charlie Wilson, the Editor of *The Times*, for letting me keep it. I wish that Mark Boxer was still alive to receive my thanks for everything he let me do on *Tatler*. So many of us who worked with him owe him our subsequent careers. I can also never repay the debt I owe to the late Christopher Dixon. Without his teaching, I dread to think what my writing would be like. I suspect it wouldn't even exist.

Finally, this collection would be little more than a few gibbering scratches if it were not for my wife, Frances. Thanks to her, I have felt cheery enough to crack whatever jokes it might be considered are contained in this slim volume. I love her and I thank her for everything.

1
THE PRELIMINARY SKETCH

*In which the Infant sketchwriter,
plucked from Obscurity by
Mr Frank Johnson, a Benefactor,
dips his little Toe in the waters of
Parliament*

MPs angling to catch the big fish

I SIT BY day in the Gallery staring down at them as they swim in and out, observing closely their bizarre habits, their attempts at communication. Microphones dangle from the end of long cables stretching down from the roof. They appear as fishing lines trailing into a large pond of inedible creatures. Often the creatures bob up and down as if preparing to bite. One of them will be allowed to remain up for long enough to talk of yet more ups and downs: employment, tax, growth rates, pay.

"Surely, surely, surely," their questions begin, closing with either "hope for the future" or "a very different story".

Their vocabulary is limited but bolstered with energetic delivery. Clichés form stepping stones over waves of uncertainty. Successes are all notable, sabres all rattled, measures all strong.

Words like "facilitate", "envisage" and "participation" indicate that a speech is pre-written. Pre-written speeches attempt to wriggle out of cliché but the attempt is usually hopeless. "Small isn't just beautiful," said Mr David Alton. "It's often better."

Mr Alton was persuading the 17 or so members who had not bothered to leave to support a motion calling for everyone to be much nicer to everyone else (The Directly Elected Neighbourhood Councils Bill).

Though a disproportionate number of members from both sides of the House bear a strong resemblance to Mr Norman Fowler, it is possible to tell young from old, left from right, senior from junior without turning them upside down. Colouring gives the first clue. Those to the right favour dark suits supplemented with a triangle of handkerchief popping from the top pocket. Those to the left – particularly the snappers – prefer weird, clashing combinations.

Young members on the right can be identified by a tendency to congratulate their seniors at regular intervals, the ritual commencing with the swift buttoning and unbuttoning of their jackets. Senior members on the right indicate their superiority by lying supine. When compelled to stand, they congratulate themselves vociferously, toying with gold pens, indicating the conclusion of their speech with the words "On line for recovery".

Members on the left, senior and junior, demonstrate no sign of any awareness of the coming oblivion predicted for them by observers. Instead, they chortle and burble merrily, signalling the termination of their thoughts with the high-pitched use of the phrase, "And they know it!".

What do they debate? Chiefly whether or not they can debate what they wish to. Topics from the outside world zip to and fro at a remarkable rate. A member from the left starts his speech with a reference to Dr Waldheim and ends it with a plea for more hospitals in Leicestershire.

Many members surprise the novice observer by their presence: the surmise of death years ago is in this way overturned. Others prove their vitality by shouting their speeches. The two parties can be differentiated less by class, weight or colouring than by their inability to share jokes.

What is the difference between an important and a minor issue? A minor issue can be readily spotted by its proposer's retort to scoffs that "This is a very serious issue".

As I write, I recall all sorts of very serious issues: assassination attempts on members, new by-passes, cats let out of bags and so on.

There was only one very serious issue on which the House was in complete accord. When the Prime Minister announced that life expectancy in the country was continuing to rise, even the most radical of radicals could think of no possible reason to condemn the news. It took a member on the right to blur the rejoicing by asking the Prime Minister whether the House had not now reached the end of its natural life.

Baffled in my observations while the creatures continue to bob, I recall yesterday's phrase from Mr Alton.

"There is no meaningful understanding of its meaning," he said of something or other. It is a phrase that rings with peculiar clarity.

1 May 1987

2
CLOTHES

A short chapter which we hope will be very attentively Perused by young Politicians who wish to Learn how to Dress, and how not to Dress

Containing a jockstrap

IT IS not every politician who manages to be pictured on the front of a Sunday newspaper dressed only in jockstrap and judge's gown. It is inevitable, then, that, among a chamber full of attention-seekers, any politician who succeeds in this objective will be subjected to a certain amount of envious ribaldry from his fellow member.

It was Mr Paul Boateng (Labour, Brent South) who, having donned this jocular garb, had found himself celebrated in no less a Sunday newspaper than the *News of the World*. All eyes, therefore, fell upon him as he waltzed his way into the Chamber while Questions to the Secretary of State for Energy dribbled to their close.

Always a snappy dresser, Mr Boateng more usually appears clothed in the style of The Chi-Lites, a popular singing group of the 1970s noted for the close formation dancing of its three backing vocalists. "Oooh-wah! Oooh-oooh-wah! Bay-bee!" are the words expected from him as he struts about the House, but more often than not the speech that emerges is rather less catchy, rather more laden with grievance.

With red and white embroidered socks, a red tie, a red and white striped shirt, a heavily shouldered-padded double-breasted suit, and hair swooping forward above his forehead in the manner of a less reticent Little Richard, Mr Boateng took his seat with no air of contrition. He was clutching a Filofax.

The theatrical theme of Sunday's photograph was pursued by Mr Dennis Skinner quoting *The Merchant of Venice* at the Secretary of State for Energy, Mr Cecil Parkinson. "The quality of mercy is not strained" crackled Mr Skinner, "It droppeth like the rain from heaven". He wished to know why mercy had not been shown to the 200 miners who had not been reinstated since the miners' strike when it had dropped so heavily on Mr Parkinson. Mr Parkinson looked avidly at the floor.

So far, so good for Mr Boateng. Had he been a Conservative rather than a Labour member, the combination of Judicial Robes, jock-strap and Filofax would have singled him out as a High Tory Freemason, and socialist conspiracy theorists would already have been attacking him. But most members on the Tory benches seemed to find nothing but healthy reassurance in the revelations of Mr Boateng's casual-wear, and for a long while not a mutter of dissent was heard.

The issue was a complicated one. Mr Boateng had dressed as a near-naked Judge not in the privacy of his own home but as part of a theatrical event: it was this public element that perplexed a number of Tories. It was inevitable that, during Questions to the Minister for the Arts, the topic should be raised

Mr Toby Jessel (Con, Twickenham) blundered to his feet, the batty Professor from a 1950s "B" movie. He blustered about having proof that the

Conservatives were much more civilized than Labour, but it appeared that he was talking of art and music becoming foundation subjects in the new education proposals. Mr Tony Banks (Lab, Newham North West) sitting next to Mr Boateng, posed the question of Clause 28. Was he worried that Mr Boateng's public performances might be curtailed by council clamp-downs on male nudity? Not a bit of it. He merely wanted the minister's assurance that the arts would not suffer damage.

Aha! Up rose Mr Boateng, happily still clad in his double-breasted suit. He asked the minister for the arts, Mr Richard Luce, a question concerning the finance of black theatre companies. "I hope he'll take this in good heart" replied Mr Luce, congenially, "but I have observed that his own artistic performances leave plenty of room for improvement".

Mr Boateng laughed sheepishly, looking downwards. Immediately, a portly Labour backbencher slid towards him to ask what on earth old Luce meant, and Mr Boateng had to explain. In a world of declining moral standards, how reassuring it is that there are still some MPs who have better things to do with their time than to sift through the Sunday papers for nude photographs of their colleagues. *16 February 1988*

Containing a vivid tie, a striped shirt, a tweed jacket and numerous watch-chains

CLOTHES can speak louder than words. This is particularly true where Mr Nicholas Soames is concerned. Though he is, by nature, loud, his clothes are often, by nature, louder. For Prime Minister's Question Time, he was wearing a shiny tie upon which the image of Superman had been superimposed. Though Mr Ian Gow (Con, Eastbourne) had, earlier in the day, requested, in no uncertain terms, that he remove the offending item, Mr Soames had shown the steely determination of his superhero in sticking to his guns.

The defiantly Scottish Mr Dennis Canavan (Lab, Falkirk West) began to complain that young Nazis in uniform had been jostled and kicked by policemen. Skilled observers, baffled by this apparent change in Mr Canavan's sympathies, discovered, after strenuous consultation, that he had actually been speaking up for young nurses in uniform.

Mr Eric Heffer rose to complain about similar police behaviour towards "priests, nuns, laity and monks". Mr Heffer was wearing a bright red tie of the type worn by many Labour members as if as a clue. But Mr Heffer somehow offsets this clue by tending towards blue and white striped shirts, the traditional uniform of the Conservative benches.

Mr Dennis Skinner, who was later to complain of British banks being "bailed out by the British taxpayer", is another socialist blue-and-white striper, and he is also the only member in the House who is always to be seen wearing a country tweed jacket. In another life, he might easily pass muster at a Hunt Ball, though his constant cries of "Maggie, Maggie, Maggie – Out, Out, Out!" might be a bit of a giveaway.

After the Prime Minister had announced changes in the administration of the Civil Service, Mr Michael Foot rose to complain. Since Christmas, Mr Foot has been sporting a bright orange tie, which, situated beneath his white-thatch hair, makes him look much like a mobile straw-hut of the type seen in exotic beach-bars in Bermuda. "One of the reasons for the low morale in the Civil Service is that she has appointed confirmed Thatcherites to the best jobs" he grunted, his tie swinging in time with his wrath.

Across the way, Mr Nicholas Fairbairn, whom unkind intimates have often accused of designing his own clothes, was clad in a shirt that seemed to have been soaked in sour Burgundy. Across his midriff, watch-chains clinked and jangled. In a previous incarnation, Mr Fairbairn may well have been the keeper of a dungeon, or, at very least, the distinguished inhabitant of one. Mr Fairbairn, it emerged, was offended by the cost of one million Labour national health brochures, which, he claimed, infringed the law. "It would be better to spend the money more charitably" he gulped, before plunging back into his seat.

Mr Tam Dalyell, dressed casually in a light blue V-neck jersey, has been quiet for some time now, perhaps brooding on the sinister facts that have still not been made public concerning the Wars of the Roses. He can usually rely on his fellow conspiracy theorist, Mr Dale Campbell-Savours, to point the necessary fingers, but Mr Campbell-Savours is at present waging a war against Mr Selwyn Gummer for his "vindictive, vicious" attacks on the Church. Dame Elaine Kellett-Bowman, who dresses with her sensible black handbag in mind, is having none of it. "At least he's giving a lead, which is more than you are" she screeched.

Elsewhere in the House, clothes are divided on a party basis. The more severe Labour members choose to wear dull ties upon which are inscribed little insignia proclaiming their allegiance to causes too serious for bright colours. The even more severe – Jeremy Corbyn, Dave Nellist – dress mainly in beards, supplemented with jackets with zips and open-necked shirts. These sartorial statements draw smoke from the ears of the older Conservative members in their pin-striped suits and brush moustaches. As for the younger Conservatives, they all look, and dress, like Mr Norman Fowler.

19 February 1988

Containing socks
of an Extra-ordinary yellowness

MR NICHOLAS Soames was wearing yellow socks.

There are days on which the wearing of yellow socks by Mr Nicholas Soames is by far the most interesting news, even though the Opposition continues to ignore all opportunities to demand a major debate on the issue.

With his unusually cheery face and well-fed body, Mr Soames can bring a smile to the most militant member, thereby disarming much anti-Government angst. Many suspect that his wearing of yellow socks is a further plot to weaken the Opposition. Mr Tony Benn will by now have gathered eagle-eyed researchers together to try to plot a line between the CIA, MI5, South Africa, the BBC and Mr Soames's yellow socks. Are Mr Soames's yellow socks in the employment of the multi-nationals? Will Mr Soames soon enter the Chamber wearing full Morris Dancing kit while Mr Ron Brown accompanies him on Mace?

The leader of the Opposition was forced to shout over the loudness of Mr Soames's socks in order to make himself heard during Prime Minister's Questions. There was an old lady in his constituency who had to live on less than £10 a week, as she had recently lost her housing benefit and was still unable to sell her house. Mr Kinnock excels when dealing with the specific:

given an old lady who is the victim of Government policies, he is acerbic, emotional and convincing; given two or more old ladies in a similar plight, he becomes verbose, half-hearted and strangely tiresome.

With her eyes turned firmly away from the glimmer of Mr Soames's socks – the colour of a canary with jaundice, perhaps, or a cowardly banana – the Prime Minister sought to reply to The Leader of the Opposition. In many ways, she is the opposite of Mr Kinnock, in that a stadium-full of old ladies brings out all her passion and eloquence, while a petulant note creeps into her voice if she is asked to talk about just one. "If there is any difficulty in that particular case. . ." she replies, pronouncing the word "particular" as if it were a form of abuse. She then advises that the victim should get in touch with the relevant department.

Aha! But, said Mr Kinnock, this victim had been in touch with the relevant department, and they had written a curt letter back. Why would the Prime Minister not change the regulations, and thus relieve "anxiety, fear and poverty"? Mr Kinnock grows increasingly like that emotional and highly successful Country and Western singer, Mr Kenny Rogers, lilting away his ballads of distress and disability, rounding them off with rollicking choruses wherein can be found a moral of tear-jerking intensity.

Sadly, the Prime Minister has revealed in the past that her favourite singer is Mr Andy Williams, who tends to eschew the crackle in the throat and the tear on the cheek in favour of the cushion on the easy chair. Pressed to give advice to Mr Kinnock's old lady, Mrs Thatcher purred that "it should not be too difficult to arrange a loan from the bank". Such advice suggests that she was wise to enter the field of politics rather than an alternative profession, such as personal counselling. With real irritation in his voice, Mr Kinnock told her that she didn't live in the real world, and asked her for the name of a building society which would leap at the idea of supplying mortgages to 73-year-olds.

Mr Kinnock returned to his seat quaking with annoyance, shaking his fists, his legs and his head in turn, a furious Basil to Mrs Thatcher's calm and all-knowing Sybil. But a kindly word from the reassuring figure of Mr Frank Dobson, combined, perhaps, with a quick glance in the direction of Mr Soames's yellow socks, soon put a smile back on his face.

It was left to Mr Tony Banks to take things a bit more seriously. He called on The Leader of the House to arrange for a debate on the Arts. He wished the House to give its advice to Lady Soames over the running of the National Theatre. And perhaps, he suggested, Lady Soames could be prevailed upon to give advice to her son upon the sensitive topic of the extraordinary yellowness of his socks.   *22 April 1988*

Containing Trousers improperly hung

MR KENNETH Clarke has the habit, not uncommon in prep-school masters, but rather more rare in politicians, of forever pulling up his trousers and re-tucking his shirt. Skilled anthropologists suggest that this can signify either some sort of personal embarrassment or a poor tailor. Now that Mr Clarke's salary is perfectly reasonable, the suggestion of a poor tailor must be discounted. This leaves personal embarrassment.

Down and up went Mr Clarke's trousers yesterday, and tuck, tuck, tuck went his hands. His personal embarrassment had become uncomfortably public. He had been expecting to deliver a message to the House confirming the British Aerospace takeover of the Rover Group. Instead, he had to deliver a message saying that British Aerospace had just told him that they hadn't quite made up their minds yet. See those trousers fall!

Mr Bryan Gould attempted to pull them off entirely, tugging at them with all his most trusted terms of condemnation. Were Mr Bryan Gould a disc jockey, he would undoubtedly be in the mould of Mr David Jacobs, easing his way into smoochy well-loved favourites in smooth, reassuring tones. Yesterday, These You Have Loved included "An Unholy Mess", "This Sorry Episode", "This Brief and Astonishing Statement" and, yes, that marvellous golden oldie from veteran bandleader Ted Heath, "The Unacceptable Face of Capitalism". As is so often the case when old tunes are played, the audience immediately dozed off.

"My statement may have been short but it was not in the least embarrassing," replied Mr Clarke, pull, pull, tuck, tuck. On this awful radio station which is to be populated by defunct politicians, Mr Clarke might well be the bluff, don't-bother-me-with-your-whining, presenter of the early-morning phone-in. Even on the best of days, he replies to Opposition members with a sort of smiling disdain, as if they are all the rough lads from the Remove without a thought in their heads.

But the Bash Street Kids were now laughing those heads off, as rough lads are prone to do. Every word uttered by Mr Clarke was greeted with uncontrolled roars of merriment, with jolly Mr Frank Dobson rocking in his seat like a toy with a spherical bottom. Things were in danger of getting out of hand and, whenever that happens, the door flies open to reveal Mr Quelch, cane a-quiver, withering remark at hand.

Mr Norman Tebbit – for it was he – pointed his finger at Mr Gould, for whom he seems to enjoy an ill-disguised contempt. Ill-disguised! Why, Mr Tebbit would never go to the trouble to disguise any contempt, preferring to parade it through the Chamber, festooned in ribbons. First, he complained of Mr Gould's "usual attitude" before complaining that "The Hon Member for Dagenham" – he enunciated the word "Dagenham" as if it were a form of household germ – "will denounce the deal whether it goes ahead or whether it doesn't".

The class seemed a little more hushed as Quelchy returned to his seat. Mr Andrew Smith (Lab, Oxford East) wished to take over Mr Gould's playlist, offering "Breathtaking Incompetence", "Mammoth Irresponsibility" and the favourite that's sweeping the dancehalls the length and breadth of the country, "Hasn't The Government Made a Mess of This?", but somehow the initial hilarity was never to return.

"You cannot reasonably cast doubts on the Government's position," said Mr Clarke, now leaning matter-of-factly on the despatch box as if it were the garden fence. With only a few minutes of interrogation to go, he seemed certain to leave the Chamber a happy man. But then the most awful thing happened. Mr Tam Dalyell chose to take his side. "Having spent 25 years involved with the motor industry, and knowing how they can change their minds at the last minute, he has my personal sympathy," he boomed. Dalyell's personal sympathy! Nothing so embarrassing had ever happened to Mr Clarke before. Tuck, tuck, pull, pull, tuck, tuck, pull, pull.

14 July 1988

3
THE 1987 GENERAL ELECTION

Containing scenes of great Humility as the Novice sketchwriter is Thrown onto the streets of Great Britain, there to witness Meetings between the Highest in the land and those they seek to Govern, involving Four Members who were soon to Lose their Seats

oo

In which Mr Roy Hattersley tucks into a Bacon and Tomato Roll

IN W H Smith's on St Pancras railway station, there were special sale offer stickers on slightly grubby books on the centre table. They included Harold Wilson's *The Governance of Britain*, Noele Gordon's *My Life At Crossroads* and Francis Pym's *The Politics of Consent*. But Mr Roy Hattersley didn't have time for browsing as he strode towards the first class compartment, conveniently situated next to the buffet. "Anything meaty, anything meaty", was his order from the buffet. Before setting his teeth into a bacon and tomato roll, he had a good sift through his brown leather executive case.

There were compartments for everything: this paper and that paper, this comb and that Parker pen, this British Caledonian First Class spongebag and that tube of Tipp-Ex. *The World at One* was about to begin. Out from the executive case came some tiny headphones which Mr Hattersley perched on his head, like two sputniks on either side of the moon.

While Mr Hattersley listened, I browsed through the Labour Party documents *Briefing to Win*. Under the section called "Environment", a particular policy caught my eye.

"I see you've got a policy on new, safer sewers", I said to his assistant, an ex-lecturer in economics.

"I don't think so", he replied, "I can't be sure but I don't *think* we've got a firm policy on that."

"Yes, you have", I replied: "Look – 'New, safer sewers'."

"Oh sewers" he said. "I thought you said Suez. We don't have a policy on Suez, but you're quite right, we do have one on sewers. They are in a terrible state."

Taking his headphones off, Mr Hattersley expounded on the news. He likes to begin his rounded sentences with either "I have long maintained. . ." or "One of my firm rules in life is that. . ."

The only news to have taken his fancy was that of the transfer of a football manager from one club to another. "I always say", he began, "that to maintain an interest in sport, it is important never to meet sportsmen."

But wasn't Brian Clough going to be with him on the platform of the Mansfield Labour Club that very afternoon? "Oh, but there are exceptions, obviously there are exceptions", he added.

"I have long maintained that anyone who likes cricket can't be all bad", he responded, with reference to Conservative supporter Tim Rice. In the car, he took pains in explaining his strong family links with the city of Nottingham. He pointed out local landmarks. ". . .and here's the crematorium", he said as a tower loomed. "No, it's the waterworks, actually,

Roy", said the local man who was driving. "Ah yes, the waterworks", said Roy. "But it does look like a crematorium, doesn't it?"

In the new borough Labour Club, red roses and beer blossomed in equal proportions. Besides Mr Hattersley on the platform sat various rose-bedecked dignatories, each introduced by Joe Ashton. ". . .And the man who tipped Coventry for the Cup – Brian Clough, and my close friend and colleague – Roy Hattersley."

But first a joke from Joe Ashton: "I sometimes think that maybe the TV programme *Who's the Greatest?* should feature Brian Clough versus Stanley Matthews one week", (pause), "and then Mrs Thatcher versus Adolf Hitler next." (Laughter). Mr Hattersley rose and began spluttering like a temperamental washing machine, chug-chug-chugging along. There were questions to be asked, he said, and one of them was this: "Do you want to give more money to the very rich or would you prefer to allow the pensioner to live in safety, comfort, or dignity?"

Safety, comfort or dignity? It seemed a wicked choice to force upon an OAP. And so back to the Inter-City 125, where, surrounded by other executives, Mr Hattersley sat well back in his seat for safety and comfort.

19 May 1987

Mr Hattersley held his seat

‿‿

Involving a Bus, Pink Paper, Sun Charm Cola and The Prime Minister; but little else

WHEN is a coach not a coach? When it is called "an advanced communications mobile office" by Conservative Central Office.

On a blustery morning, the world's Press was bussed to a windswept site in London's Docklands, there to view the new phenomenon that is the Prime Minister's mobile campaign headquarters. For three-quarters of an hour, photographers pointed their cameras at it, noted that it was blue, noted also that it bore the slogan "Moving Forward with Maggie", stared at it and stared at it again. Perhaps we all thought that, in this toytown environment, it would open its mouth at the front and start giving us the latest figures on health and unemployment.

"That we should be reduced to this. . .", one leading political commentator said to another as they both pushed open the door to the coach's loo. Other reporters, worried that they might be missing out on a scoop, squeezed in too. "Pink paper." They all wrote it down on their pads. Someone else opened the small fridge. Mrs Thatcher will be existing on an exclusive diet of something called "Sun Charm Cola".

Meanwhile, Harvey was blaring through a megaphone at the journalists who were still preparing for their voyage into the advanced communications mobile office. "This is a vehicle we've implemented to a high level of communication specification", he said. "The Prime Minister will be able to sit at her table, telephone in hand, and watch TV."

"Thanks, Harvey", Roger said to Harvey as Harvey handed Roger the megaphone. Such a slick switchover suggested that Roger and Harvey had been introducing people to buses for most of their professional lives. "Driver Ron Sharp was with us on the last campaign and we'd like to welcome him on board", Roger said.

At last, the Prime Minister's black Daimler drew up. "Right, now here we are", she said as she stepped out of the car.

"What did she say? What did she say?" asked journalists at the back of the 20-strong throng. "Right, now here we are."

How many different versions of that important statement were beamed by satellite throughout the world? Will "Right now, here we are" go to Germany, "Right! Now hear! We are!" to Japan, and "Write now, hear we 'ah'," to the United States? It was certainly the most important thing she said all morning.

The Prime Minister posed at the wheel, talking through her frozen smile in a manner reminiscent of Postman Pat. "Yes, it is jolly cold isn't it" and "Full-steam ahead".

Her husband, Denis, said little but smiled genially, "Ah yes" was his most extensive comment on anything, "Ah yes".

The journalists and cameramen then got back into their buses and followed the advanced communications mobile office as it wheeled its way around the Docklands. Inside the headquarters of the Dockland Development Corporation small groups of journalists were ushered into a room to see, for a few seconds each, Mrs Thatcher sipping coffee. Afterwards, one journalist read out to the others the notes he had taken. 'She said that she was proud that it had attracted 300,000 million from the private sector. . .''

"That's billion, surely," another said. "3 billion".

"300,000 billion" wrote another.

Figures are already going by the board. The election is becoming like a disc jockey's breakfast, with each party striving to outdo the others by talking modern, modern, modern. And, for the Conservatives, Harvey ("Thanks, Roger") and Roger ("Thanks, Harvey") are used to it. To them, this election is just another advanced communications mobile drivers' holiday.   *22 May 1987*

In which a Little Lad says Hello before His Constituents Bid him Farewell

"IT'S ME!" says 5ft 3in Peter Bruinvels, peering over a red garden gate, "The Little Lad from the House of Commons!"

Bruinvels was elected the Conservative Member of Parliament for Leicester East in 1983 with a majority of just 933. Out canvassing in 1987, he emphasizes two things: his height ("I'm the shortest Tory MP: nice to know you're getting an individual and not just a yes man, eh?") and his Strong Stands.

In the car on the way to a factory, he told me more about his Strong Stands. He has campaigned against Sunday trading and diplomatic immunity, against video nasties being shown in prisons and against homosexuality being taught in schools. He is also against abortion, women deacons and all forms of surrogacy. "By voting for me, you don't get a yes man – you get a personality", he tells voters.

But he feels most strongly of all about capital punishment, which, together with the retention of the red telephone box, is one of the things he is For. "On my very first day in the Commons I tabled a motion on the return of the death penalty for terrorists. I then said I'd pull the lever myself, and that got me a lot of publicity in the national Press, an awful lot."

Recently, a woman came up to him and said: "I want your second job." He replied that he had only one – he was a full-time MP. She said: "No, I want to be the hangman too." He chortled at the recollection. "We're getting a lot of support on that."

"I'm very much people-orientated", he says as he nips from house to house and he is very cheery as he tells householders just what he thinks of "Labour's Go-Gay policies", and Leicester's twinning with Nicaragua. "How long have you lived here for?" he asks and when the reply comes he says "Good gracious!" He then says that he's "very much a Leicester-Leicester man", adds another joke about his height, encourages a Conservative vote, and moves on.

Between houses he expands on the death penalty, always ready to interrupt the dissertation with a wave and a friendly smile for a passerby. "Life doesn't mean life. I want to see the punishment fit the crime. Afternoon! Lovely day! In my election address, I say that prison is too good for some people.

"How's the garden? Good! I mean, three good meals a day, colour television and, until recently, they had porno videos in prison, but I put a stop to that. Hello, I'm Peter Bruinvels, the Little Lad from the House of Commons!"

His new Labour opponent is an Asian called Keith Vaz. "Vaz is making the mistake of concentrating his efforts on the black community or as I prefer to call them, the ethnic community." There has been a recent case in Leicester of an Asian family being housed at the cost to the ratepayer of £695 per week. "I don't like the wogs", says a Conservative voter on the doorstep. Bruinvels nods. It is not a term employed by the Little Lad from the House of Commons, who calls it "the rude word beginning with W". He prefers to call them "our friends from overseas".

We call in at the Ex-Cell-O factory ("How long have you worked here for? Good gracious!"). He points at his rosette as he says to each worker, "I'm your MP". They know. They have seen him on television. "I like being on television", he replies, "and I'm on a lot, aren't I?! You see, I'm not a yes man – I'm a nuisance!"

He swings to and fro on his heels as he tells of his new campaign to make the unemployed do community service. "People putting their noses in the trough should work for it – always causes a hoo-haa when I say it though!" And on he scampers, the Little Lad from the House of Commons, for the death penalty, against teaching homosexuality in our schools.

27 April 1987

Mr Bruinvels lost his seat by 1,924 votes to the Labour candidate

∞∞

Containing Jaunty scenes in which Mr Benn expresses much interest in Thomas the Tank Engine

THE THEME music from *Chariots of Fire* booms through megaphones on the top of a parked car. As the music fades, it makes way for a familiar voice.

"This is Tony Benn. Don't forget June 11th. Use your vote. Vote for the old. Vote for the young. Vote for the sick. Vote for peace. This is Tony Benn. . ."

In fact, it isn't Tony Benn at all, but a tape recording of Tony Benn. Tony Benn himself is elsewhere in Chesterfield. The tape recorder is helping him achieve his great purpose of keeping personalities, in this case his own, out of politics.

A Labour Party worker takes up the megaphone. "Despite what the Press tell you, he doesn't eat children and he doesn't bite dogs. He's an ordinary man. Come along and shake hands with him and say hello."

A while later, Tony Benn is there in person, making a five minute speech through the megaphone in the direction of a shopping precinct. He combines a pleasantly scout-masterish vocabulary – he talks of "bobbies" and "coppers" and "making a go of it" and "in the old days" – with an almost mystical ability to see the conspiracy in things.

In those five minutes, he links closing down the coal pit to supporting apartheid, Peter Wright to tax cuts for the very rich, the Tories using the police as a private army to cuts in the NHS, and all of them to "a government which is trying to keep us in a state of fear, and the moment we escape from that fear we will have a better country to live in".

By the time he has finished speaking, a number of elderly people have gathered around, smiling and nudging each other. Abandoning his megaphone, he approaches them, pipe in hand. "How old are you? You're not! Well, that's a good age!" The recipient of the compliments, a Labour voter all his life, urges a return to the death penalty. Prisons, he argues, are holiday camps. Benn listens hard. "Well, prisons are very overcrowded, aren't they?" says Benn, looking for common ground.

"Make 'em a lot less crowded by bringing back hanging", replies the man.

Benn says he would like to see the bobby back on the beat to give a cuff round the ear to high spirited youngsters. The man agrees.

Puffing at his pipe, jangling the change in his pocket, Benn calls at a council house. An old woman points to a small amount of grass growing between the paving stones. The council hasn't done anything about it and she could take a tumble.

"I wonder if weed killer would do the trick?" Benn suggests.

She's already tried Domestos, she complains.

Tony Benn has fought no less than 15 Parliamentary elections, and he obviously enjoys talking to his constituents. He thinks there should be annual general elections "to keep government on its toes".

He is himself a victim of some of his conspiracy theories. "They couldn't defeat me in Bristol so they abolished my seat", he says. "And now I have sought political asylum in Chesterfield."

His chat is jaunty and peculiarly old fashioned. At moments, he could be the vicar in an Ealing comedy. A woman says that her husband is a gents hairdresser and Benn talks with astonishment of seeing a pigtail on a man. A child is reading a book called *The Twits* and he asks her if she has ever read *Thomas The Tank Engine*.

He has the ability to find political inspiration in the most mundane complaints. He approaches two old women and asks them about the state of the country. They complain about the dog droppings everywhere. He pauses, puffing his pipe in sympathy. "When they say there is no work to be done, it is nonsense really, isn't it, when there are all those fouled paths to be cleaned up."

He is a great optimist, often talking of "hope for the future". He also finds hope in the immediate past, forgetting calls for the death penalty and trouble with dog droppings when he looks back on the day. "So many people come up to me and say 'Isn't there a chance of peace in the Gorbachev disarmament proposals?'" he reports merrily.   *28 May 1987*

Mr Benn held his seat

In which Mr Cyril Smith buys a Modest Luncheon

"**M**AY I jump the queue for a couple of frankfurters, girls?"
"Have you got the sausages, Cyril?"
"Just getting them, mother."

Cyril Smith was out shopping for his dinner before getting down to proper canvassing in the afternoon. He was striding in front through Rochdale market, while his younger brother Norman, up until last week the Lord Mayor of Rochdale, was pushing their 83-year-old mother in her wheelchair behind.

First stop was Billy Duff Cooked Meats. "A bit of tongue, no, make that two bits, and not too thin. You've cut it thick have you? Good lad!" After buying half a pound of beef spread, the three moved to Collins' Biscuits Stall. "Hiya girls!" "Hello Cyril!" They all wanted Liberal stickers for their lapels.

Cyril ordered some Walkers Shortbread, Chocolate Chips, Almond Cookies, and "mix us a pound of chocolate biscuits, love."

"What you doin', Cyril?" said his mother from her wheelchair.

"Just getting the chocolate biscuits, mother."

"Don't forget the chocolate biscuits!" replied his mother.

"And give me a pound of mixed creams."

"What you doin'?"

"Getting a pound of mixed creams."

"Are we all right for cream crackers?"

"Jacobs or Crawfords, mother?"

"Jacobs."

Putting eight different packets of biscuits into his carrier bag, Cyril strode on. Everyone seemed to recognize him, and, more unusually for a politician, he recognized them. "Aye! Aye!" he would say in passing to youngsters, "how are ye, old son?" to the older generation.

A woman came up and said that her daughter had got a job as registrar at the college. "Ah, we went to tea there, mother," said Cyril. "I said, we went to tea there. D'y'remember?"

Like many people, she told Cyril she'd be voting for him. "That's kind of you, love," he said. "Tell you what, come half past ten Sunday to a great big rally if you want – David Steel, Shirley Williams, five other Liberals. Be smashin'."

The procession came to a halt as mother chatted to a lady friend from her days when she cleaned the town hall. To one side, the friend's daughter asked Cyril how his mother was. "She's proud of you, she's proud of both of you. And every reason to be!"

Cyril then got chatting to a young woman in a wheelchair about her disability allowance, saying cheerio with "well done, love. Keep goin', kid."

And on to the Bacon Stall. "They never have trotters now, do they, Norman?" Cyril shouted back to Norman. "No, they never have trotters now," agreed Norman. "Do I usually have creamy or crumbly?" he asked the girl serving the cheese. "Crumbly, Cyril."

More cheese from Jill's Cheese Pantry. "Some gorgonzola, please, love. D'ye'sell chutney? A jar of chutney, oh, and a jar of pickles, and one of your Stiltons."

An elderly woman recalled her recent golden wedding anniversary party. "It were all right, weren't it, kid?" said Cyril.

He stopped at Stocks sweet stall. "What sort of toffees do you want, mother?"

"I'm all right with toffees."

Cyril bought a quarter of chocolates for himself and squeezed them into one of the two carrier bags.

An old man came up and shook Cyril's hand. "Last time I saw you was at Fred Kershaw's funeral," he said. "Aye," said Cyril, holding him by the shoulder. "Fred and I used to play together as kids."

Two young women passed by eating sticky buns. "You'll finish up like me, girls!" said Cyril. They giggled and walked on.

Norman and mother had got chatting to someone else. "Come on. I'm movin' now, Norman, or I won't get me dinner in time, so I shan't get out campaignin' this afternoon!" shouted Cyril.

On the way out, the smell of hot potatoes from Ye Olde Lancashire Oven was too much to bear. "Tell you what," said Cyril, "we'll 'ave a bag of those for our dinner too."   *30 May 1987*

Mr Smith held his seat

∞∞∞

Containing Scenes of great Sorrow as Gentleman Jenkins begs for Votes

HIS GRUBBY old coat battered by the fierce Glasgow wind, the old gent stands hatless in the pouring rain. To the shoppers who emerge from the Presto supermarket in Byers Road, he can offer nothing more than an outstretched hand and a ready smile.

Within the dry, well-lit interior of Presto, a Harp Lager Beer Bonanza is in full swing. Lyons mini pies are reduced to 39p and Presto Whole Orange Drink is just 49p. But these bargains are not for the old gent. The rain is his only roof, the kindness of strangers his only joy as he goes about his purpose. "Vair nice to meet you", he shouts after shoppers as they scuttle away from him, bags laden, back to the warmth of their hearthsides.

"I hope I may have your support," he begs as they dash, "I hope I may have your support." He could tell them of better days, if only they'd listen. He could tell them of days of wine and without roses, of days when he was Chancellor of the Exchequer, president of the European Economic Community, leader of the Social Democratic Party – the lot. But they have no time to spare as they rush through the rain.

"Hello, I'm Roy Jenkins," he says to an old lady standing by the Presto bus stop. "Are you waiting for a bus?" Soliciting conversation from lonely old women! That it should come to this! It is as if Ralph McTell had never lived, as if the caring and compassionate society were nothing but a forgotten dream. "Vair nice to have met you," he shouts after her as she hastens onto her bus.

The howling of the wind and the slashing of the rain may bite at his old brown coat, but nothing can batter his pride. His own silk handkerchief peeps out of his outer pocket. His black shoes, now flecked by the years, were once the very best that money could buy. He keeps his mind alert by approaching strangers and asking them where they live. If he can keep them talking, he surmises, they might not throw him out.

The Glaswegians of Hillhead are a friendly people. They tell the gent their addresses. "I know it, I know it," he replies, and then gives them full details of how to get there. They already know, of course, but there's no point in upsetting him.

Occasionally, he'll get the odd one who wants to take the discussion further, who won't stop at giving the gent his address and occupation, who frankly wants trouble. A man tells him that unemployment has always been with us. He tries to argue back, but the man won't stop. "You won't keep quiet for a moment," says the gent. The man continues. "Well, that's not the view I would take," says the gent. But still the man rants. "Vair nice to meet you anyway," says the gent, moving on.

Like many people in his situation, the gent really just wants someone who'll lend a friendly ear. He's not so good at listening himself, and why should he be? While an old woman goes on about the wee problem of the ugly awnings of the hairdresser's shop next door, his right hand strokes the bottom half of his face, as if signalling contemplation. As an Asian complains of roads that need repairing, the gent jiggles his left hand up and down, restless for a solution or, at the very least, an escape.

The bright lights of the Presto supermarket cruelly illuminate the puddles on the pavement. Gentleman Jenkins has been on this patch for five long years, and now they're threatening to move him on. It's not right. "I hate the dividedness in this country," a stranger told him. "You've put your finger on the core," he replies. He has to be grateful even for cores, these days.

Sometimes, you can see his mind wandering away from the problem at hand, away from the awnings and the bus stops and the road repairs to the days of long ago. Glaswegians, however cheery, are apt to come too close and poke him with their fingers while expounding on a paradox, and he is not used to such unguarded physicality. Like a member of the royal family, he releases himself by taking one step backwards, smiling, shaking their hands and saying: "Vair nice to meet you," his eyes already looking for a new friend.

Later in the day, he finds shelter in the Whiteinch Community Centre on Dumbarton Road. There he parts with a dirty old ten pence piece for a ticket for the bottle stall. He examines a bottle of Bulgarian red. Might it some day be his? Alas, his number does not come up. He retreats onto the streets of Glasgow, still managing a smile. It's a tough life, but a good one.

1 June 1987

Mr Jenkins lost his seat. He is now Lord Jenkins of Hillhead

∞∞

In which the Sketchwriter, finding himself in Northern Ireland, chances upon Mr Enoch Powell, a Megaphone, and a Classical allusion in the shadow of a Supermarket

ENOCH Powell's fingers have not touched the button of a cordless telephone, and his lips remain unbesmirched by the cheeks of babies. He doesn't even believe in knocking on doors and asking people where they live. "You can't possibly do a door-to-door canvass with 72,000 constituents", he reports.

Yesterday was his first week of campaigning in South Down. "I always start on this week", he says. I saw him at a roundabout in the town of Downpatrick, holding a microphone, giving an election address and driving, all at the same time.

"Good morning Downpatrick! Good morning Downpatrick!" he was saying rather in the manner of the man employed in pantomimes to get children going.

"You have your opportunity to do your bit for Ulster. For 20 years the province has known nothing but uncertainty. When the government stops playing around with Anglo-Irish agreements and that sort of thing we will have peace and security in Northern Ireland. We mean to have a secure future. Tell them we mean to have a secure future. They'll listen. They'll have to listen. They know they'll have to listen."

Behind his car was a red Ford with bulletproof glass, a reinforced undercarriage and two plain clothes policemen. I caught up with Mr Powell in a cul-de-sac. "What can I do for you?" he asked me through his

[27]

megaphone. The words boomed out on to the Downpatrick housing estate.

Mr Powell is now 74 years old. His expression is so alert and his eyes so beady that his face looks like that of a young actor who has been made up rather heavy handedly – thick lines, grey moustache, whitening in the hair – to give the impression of age. He speaks as if dictating a word-perfect letter to an erudite but difficult councillor. How long has he been in politics? "If you would like to say I have been in politics for 40 years you will not be over-estimating."

His election photograph is unrepentently uningratiating. His eyes stare away from the camera. His mouth remains entirely horizontal. His post box message mentions no wife, no children, no grandchildren, no past achievements. It concerns itself solely with the failure of the government to grant the people of Ulster the rights accorded to them in 1922. "In 1985, they were brutally repudiated by the Anglo-Irish agreement." In his election poster, Powell's face glares out of a Union Jack.

Later in the morning, I witnessed what might well have been the fastest walkabout in election history. Mr Powell got out of his car, walked briskly into the Superite Prices supermarket, shook two women by the hand, made one of his slightly grisly beams at a check out girl, and zipped back out again. The entire walkabout lasted no more than 90 seconds.

Had Mr Kinnock been there, he would have started strumming a frozen cod; Mrs Thatcher would have asked a boil in the bag chicken exactly where it lived and the two Davids would have agreed publicly and unanimously over their decision to purchase an oven-ready shepherd's pie for two. But Mr Powell made no attempt at jollity until well away, and then it was in Greek.

Asked if he would win the election, he said, "We cannot foretell the future, as Solon said to Croesus," and then added, as an aid to journalists, "a typical classical allusion from Mr Powell". His headmasterly jests are lent additional punch by the incongruity of the fierce chiselled features of their exponent: it is as if Zeus had just told a knock-knock joke.

On the supermarket forecourt, he allowed himself a couple of minutes to admonish Mrs Thatcher and the "evil of the Anglo-Irish agreement. . .I accused her of treachery. It is a word she has not forgotten. She knows that she did wrong and she knew she was doing wrong when she did it. You had only to watch her face to see the truth in what I say."

And then it was back to his car and his megaphone. "Good morning Downpatrick! Tell the Government to stop mucking about! The only way ahead for Ulster is the Union. The Union is for everybody and about everybody. . ."

Waiting for Mr Powell outside the Saintfield Orange Hall was a party worker. He admired Maggie, he said, but she was too half-hearted about terrorism. He thought that they should pop their heads off, like they did in Malaya. Perhaps it is small wonder that gimmicks in Ulster are so few.

2 June 1987

Mr Powell lost his seat

What passed between Mr Denis Healey and a man he claimed to be a Liar, told in Comical fashion

IT HAS been said that television is killing off the strong music hall tradition of the Labour Party, but Denis Healey, that grand old man of seaside piers and party conferences, is still making 'em roll in the aisles.

Out in Cardiff, he went down a storm. He makes you laugh before he even opens his mouth; that's his magic. With his face as red as a chimp's posterior, and brows that make you think a couple of squirrels are hibernating in his eyes, you can't help but smile.

And this season he's added a couple of red roses to his get-up. They're plastic through and through. "They don't wilt on television", he chortles.

Dirty Denis warmed up the Cardiff crowd with a few "Doctor, Doctor" jokes. "Alliance supporters have suffered a mortal blow", he said at the morning's press conference. Then he paused – timing's everything, you understand – before adding: "Dr David Owen has shackled them to Mrs Thatcher's chariot wheels." Boom! Boom!

After a couple more "Doctor, Doctor" jokes, including "fatuous impudence" and "future Tory Prime Minister", the audience was eating out of the palm of his hand. Just the time for one or two jokes of the Blue variety. Old Geoffrey Howe, the specialist trouser-dropping act, had been in town earlier.

"I was very surprised to hear that Geoffrey has attacked me. Geoffrey is always a nice, if (pause) rather subdued fellow. Finding him attacking me is rather like (pause) stepping on a hearth rug and hearing it squeak!!!" Every one a gem!

And the Blue jokes kept on coming. Cleaner comedians on the circuit have ignored the hanky panky of Keith and Harvey, but not our Dirty Denis. When someone mentioned the pranksters in his own party, Dirty Denis quipped back with talk of "a number of Conservative candidates shuffling off to jail for various forms of delinquency". Boom! Boom!

The Second Act was for the radio audience. "I was going to call you gorgeous but then I realized that was sexist", he chirped to the radio girl. For a moment, he looked like Mr Marvo flirting with his sequinned assistant. Would he then put her into a box and cut her up?

Between acts, Dirty Denis took a well-earned rest from the glare of the floodlights and the smell of greasepaint to tell me a thing or two about the way he puts his show together. It seems that the Geoffrey Howe Squeaky Hearth Rug crack was an adaptation of his Geoffrey Howe Dead Sheep gag from way back, and he got that one from Winston who called Attlee a dead lamb. This one will run and run.

And so the curtains rolled back for the third and final act, set in a pedestrian precinct. The familiar opening scene had young and old approaching Dirty Denis singing either "I've Been a Labour Voter All My Life" or "You're A Great Man, Sir".

Then Dirty Denis picked up the megaphone. "When Sir Geoffrey Howe was here this morning it was pouring with rain", he began, "but now the sun is shining and on June 11 the sun will be shining all over the country". Boom! Boom!

For his last trick, he performed a walkabout, a potentially dangerous stunt involving the possibility of coming face to face with a member of the public. "Mrs T only talks to dogs and ducks", he quipped.

But then the unthinkable happened, and someone disagreed with him. "I was in the forces when you were minister for defence", said the ordinary member of the public, "and you shouldn't be planning to leave this country defenceless".

Dirty Denis looked cross, an emotion he signals, like so many in the political road show, by smiling. Would he give this ne'er do well a squirt of the rose?

After a thirty second discussion he rounded on him, telling him he was a liar, and had never been in the services. The man replied that he had been in Aden. Dirty Denis told him again that he was a liar, and strode off ready to shoot the punchline over his shoulder. "Drop dead!" he shouted, and again "drop dead!" The Old Farceur Goes to War. Ah, they don't make 'em like that any more.

4 June 1987

Mr Healey held his seat

<hr/>

∞∞∞

In which the Sketchwriter, a trifle exhausted, appears to grow Tetchy while following The Prime Minister into a Fun-Fair

EXTENDING her campaign policy of restricting her exclusive interviews to those inquisitive people between the ages of three and five, Mrs Margaret Thatcher went straight for the nappy-wearing voter with a trip to "kiddies korner" at the Alton Towers theme park, Staffordshire.

Conservative strategists have determined that children aged three will be able to vote in the year 2002, when Mrs Thatcher will be entering her fifth term of office as Prime Minister. By that time, many old-age pensioners of today will be disenfranchized owing to death, whilst those waiting in national health queues for major operations will be only a couple of years away from their hospital bed, and thus too excited to rock the boat. By 2002, the unemployed will have grown used to it, and the school leaver will be unable to spell "X", so today's nappy-wearer must obviously be the main target of any far-sighted political party.

With this in mind, the tour kicked off with a demonstration of dancing hydraulic diggers. The factory organizers, all in Redcoat blazers, kept the press at bay while a hideous five-minute medley of well-known classical hits set to a rock beat blared out and the vast machines began their strangely obscene "dance", now lifting up their scoops, now pirouetting, now coming to a happy close.

Denis was delighted. "Fabulous!" he exclaimed while the clumsy vehicles turned turtle to a reggae version of the *1812 Overture*. "Best thing I've ever seen," he assured the managing director as he left.

This was, of course, a "photo opportunity", for possible inclusion in *Dandy* and *June and Schoolfriend*. "What about the unemployed, Mrs Thatcher?" shouted a spoilsport reporter as she beetled past. "Tremendous, terribly clever," replied Mrs Thatcher, beaming.

Press etiquette dictates that if one aids the editor of *Dandy* in the morning, then one is duty-bound to award the editor of *Tiny Tots* with a photo opportunity in the afternoon. Alton Towers proved splendid for the purpose. The Prime Minister was greeted by a man dressed in pink frills with a floppy Gertrude Shilling-style hat.

Was this a disgraced former Cabinet minister taking his first tentative steps towards rehabilitation in the eyes of the public? No, it was Stuart Hall, the ex-television personality, although his fawning presence was never explained.

Unfortunately, Central Office had not reckoned with the fact that on Thursday afternoons, the disgruntled unemployed constitute a fair part of the population of Alton Towers. While she boarded the Skyride Luxury Gondola and travelled over Fantasy World, she was followed by yells of "Evil Thatcher" and less reticent exclamations.

Disembarking from the gondola, she caught sight of a member of her target group. "Hello, and what is your favourite ride?" she asked a boy aged four. "Football," he replied. Aha, a tricky customer! "Oh! Is there football at Alton Towers?" asked the Prime Minister, quite happy to indulge in the cut and thrust of Kiddie Politics. "No, but there is at home," replied the boy, undoubtedly a future recruit for Militant Tendency.

After this bout of Catch-the-Child, Mrs Thatcher passed Pepe's Tuck Shop Potato Bar, three jugglers, two men on stilts, Henry the Dog and the Grand Canyon Rapids, and entered Josiah Wedgewood's workshop after glancing in the window of Toys Fair (at a Princess of Power doll.)

Emerging from Josiah Wedgewood's workshop, Mrs Thatcher caught sight at last of the corps of grown-ups who had been following her, unnoticed, all day. Bravely ignoring the kiddy vote she allowed them a couple of minutes to question her.

"Is this really a suitable venue for an election campaign?" asked a clever-clogs grown-up. "Yes, indeed. . ." began the Prime Minister, but as she was about to continue, toytown news blared out from the Henry The Dog machine. It seems that a chocolate and toffee trail has led investigators to a friendly ghost called Charlie. That's the kind of good news Britain so sorely needs. *5 June 1987*

Containing Mellow scenes with Mr Freud followed by a Babe-in-arms experiencing a Kiss from Mr Jeffrey Archer

I T WAS a sunny day and a middle-aged woman with no shoes on wandered over to Clement Freud. "When we are the Government," said Mr Freud, "everybody will have shoes."

His approach to campaigning is mellow. While walking along the main street of the town of March with him, I had to keep reminding him that he was meant to be electioneering. He then tentatively approached a shopper (he has no need to introduce himself) and, after a bit of chat and another nudge, he would just manage to say: "I wonder whether you would support me on Thursday," in the manner of one politely asking for a second lump of sugar.

Everyone we spoke to seemed to be voting for him already. I was keen to witness a confrontation, so he allowed me to select his targets. I asked him to canvass in a gun-shop. The owner, it turned out, was voting Liberal. "Your name is sonynymous with the Fens," he explained. "Synonymous," corrected Mr Freud, picking up a banana, "and what do you shoot with this?"

He admitted that he had not taken much part in the national campaign. He had been down to Southend once, but that was about all. He likes the uncaring approach of the Southend Liberal. "He beats people over the head with his clip-board."

Looking for a likely Conservative household, I moved him towards a neat house with fancy net curtains and garden ornaments. He offered odds of 7–4 that it was Conservative; "but you really know it is a Conservative house when there are two cars parked outside and both of them have road tax discs".

The occupier, dressed in black tie and dinner jacket, was in fact voting for Freud. "You've done me a good turn, and now I'll do you a good turn," he explained.

We came across a number of people who had been done good turns by Freud. "You see, I don't want to be a minister. I like my constituency very much more than Westminster. I like these people."

He has a merry band of young canvassers enthusiastically doling out his stickers – "CF MP OK", "Clement Freud Works", and "I Will Vote Clement Freud When I'm 18" – but he himself favours a more deadpan approach. "Have I done enough yet?" he asked me after he had knocked on five or six doors.

In the afternoon March was invaded by Jeffrey Archer on his 92nd constituency of the campaign. In between signing autographs, he stood on the back of a Land-Rover and energized through a microphone. "In Margaret Thatcher we have found the greatest leader since Winston Churchill . . .if we have to resort to armed resistance you can be quite sure that the Resistance leaders will be Conservative chairmen."

Afterwards, Archer called everyone by their Christian names ("Are we gonna win then, Albert?") and enthused about the "outstanding" Tory candidate, Malcolm. Meanwhile, the red-tied Labour candidate shouted through a megaphone: "Mrs Thatcher can have an operation whenever she wants. She can have one on a Monday, she can have one on a Tuesday, she can have one on a Wednesday. . ."

As Jeffrey Archer posed by a baby in a pram, an elderly man criticized Malcolm's view on capital punishment. "He's all for it," said a Conservative. "Yes, but only in certain circumstances," complained the elderly man.

But Clement Freud's mind was on other things. Next Saturday he will throw a party – though he doesn't know yet whether it will be a wake or a celebration. Few, if any, MPs will be invited. He's not very MP-minded, though David Steel has campaigned for him in Ely. "We had him drive through. We negotiated that he sat in the window seat. He arrived late, and I missed the Derby. First Derby I've missed in 25 years."   *8 June 1987*

Mr Freud lost his seat to the Conservative candidate

∞∞∞

In which a piece of Nougat finds itself halfway into the Mouth of Lord Whitelaw

"PLEASED to meet you very nice seeing you hello Willie Whitelaw how are you nice speaking to you hello Willie Whitelaw jolly good pleased to meet you."

No time-and-motion expert could devise a means whereby Lord Whitelaw could shake more hands in a shorter time. He darted around Dewsbury market yesterday in five minutes, telling about 100 people how pleased he was to meet them.

His method brooks no appeal: the tone in which he says "Pleased to meet you" signals a simultaneous goodbye. When he told a member of the public that he hoped they'd vote Conservative, and the man replied "No", he answered "Well, think about it, jolly good", and then, to a new face, "Hello, Willie Whitelaw, pleased to meet you."

Similarly, when another person said "A lot of people are worried about education", he replied genially, "Quite right too, jolly good, hello, Willie Whitelaw, pleased to meet you."

In his brown tweed suit, he speaks to passers-by with the air of a benevolent landowner wishing the staff a happy new year. His most frequent expressions are "jolly good", "gracious me" and "but there we are" (as in "I'm afraid we've never really managed to get the West Indian vote, but there we are").

When he talks of politics, he does so in that melodic stream of consciousness peculiar to the landed gentry. "Of course people try and play tricks on you at these times, have scares and so on, but do people really want to go back to secondary picketing, do people really want to be ruled by all these left-wingers, because everybody can't have it, nobody can have it – is that really the way we want to carry on, for goodness sake, let's not throw all our achievements away or that would be a disaster."

The width of his enthusiasm is boundless. As we scaled up a dark brick staircase in Batley he exclaimed, "I say, this is rather marvellous, isn't it?" At the top of the stairs was a sweet factory. The owner explained that a combination of luck and initiative was responsible for their success.

"Fascinating performance, isn't it? Marvellous," replied Willie. The owner explained that he was shortly going to Hemel Hempstead to view a hamburger machine with a view to adapting it to make truffles. "Gracious me!" said Willie. He was then introduced to some of the female workforce. "How long have you worked here?" "Five months." "Jolly good! And you?" "Eight years." "Have you really!" "I was originally from Manchester." "Manchester! My goodness me!"

At times he is reminiscent of Alastair Sim. A photographer told him that he wouldn't fit into the picture because he was too tall. "Too tall, am I? Deary me. Well, there we are. Jolly good."

He had vowed twice "I must not eat" but a photographer persuaded him to hold a nougat half way into his mouth. Could he move the position of his hand, asked the photographer. "Well, I hold them like this usually, but there we are," he replied, changing position. "Just one more photograph," said the photographer. "It's always just one more, but there we are." Realizing the only escape, Willie popped the whole nougat into his mouth and swallowed it. "There. Can't do any more now, can we?" he said, and then, to the owner, "Mmmm, very good actually, terribly good, awfully good."

And so to a warehouse packed with Masters of the Universe Jelly Coated Novelties, Strawberry-Flavoured Boot Laces, Slime Slurps, Rum-Flavoured Balls and many other varieties. "Lovely goodies here, I must say," he said.

There was a final demand for a photograph of him holding a bundle of gold and silver bubble-gum coins. The photographer poured too many into his hands, and they spilt. "Oh, lord," he said as they tinkled on to the ground. "Deary me. O, well. Jolly good."

His sweet factory tour over, he looked ahead to the next few days. On Tuesday he visits Liverpool. "Dead loss for us, I'm afraid," he said. "But there we are."   *6 June 1987*

4
THE PRIME MINISTER AND THE LEADER OF THE OPPOSITION

Concerning two People who do not Hit it Off

In which Mr Neil Kinnock is sighted upon Home Territory

COMING to the platform to accept her merit award, Mrs Catherine Griffiths proved that it is still possible to gain unanimous applause from a Labour Party Conference, so long as one is aged 102, trained as a nurse, the child of a miner and 69 years a Labour Party member. Others, particularly leaders, find it more difficult.

"Those were the days when people had to fight for their rights", she said, clutching her rose-embossed wall plaque. "I had to fight for my rights. Those were the days."

To her right, Roy Hattersley manoeuvred a bandaged finger hither and thither along his capacious mouth as if pondering whether it might taste rather nicer with the addition of a tot of *sauce Hollandaise*. Elsewhere on the platform, all were beams and smiles. Even Mr Dennis Skinner, who generally looks uncharacteristically unhappy and responsible in his elevated position on the platform, was seen to clap. But it would be his last applause for over an hour. Mr Kinnock was due to speak.

Mr Kinnock has only to clear his throat at a cocktail party for commentators to observe that he is about to make one of the most important speeches of his political career. The most important speech of his career is now becoming such a regular occurrence that it now follows a set pattern: a word or two about whatever is the most recent bad news for the party and then he says, voice aquiver: "But out of defeat, we must build victory!"

Lest this be too provocative an opinion for all sides of the party to swallow, he adds: "Yes, we were defeated – but we certainly weren't beaten." And then, smiling a brief and jagged smile, swinging the top half of his body as if in rehearsal for a head-butt, he shouts: "Let's be candid". Candid is an ancient Welsh term meaning evasive, blustering or long-winded, as in the expression "Welsh Labour Candidate".

"There are many lessons to learn", he said, controversially. "And we shall learn them." Mr Eric Heffer in the audience looked like the man who first put the grunt into disgruntled.

Mr Kinnock began to detail the views that bound the great movement together and which would never, but never, be abandoned. These were – in no particular order – liberty, democracy, justice, security, opportunity and disagreement.

He then reached the first port in his storm: ". . .regardless of sex, race, colour or creed". So saying, he swung his head to the right and looked purposefully into the middle distance, ever the benevolent god. Immediately to his left, Mr Tam Dalyell sat with his body lurching away, an old sea dog resisting a fierce westerley wind.

With his wistful smile, Mr Kinnock remembered the question Mr Ron

Todd had asked two months ago: "What do you say to a docker who earns £400 a week, owns his house, a new car, microwave and video; as well as a small place near Marbella?"

Two obvious answers swept through the minds of delegates. One was: "You are a liar." The second: "You are in heavy debt". The only other possible response might be: "You are under arrest."

But this was to misinterpret the thrust of Mr Kinnock's argument: he was sticking up for that underprivileged and neglected section of the Labour community, the blissfully happy. Alternately indignant and high-spirited, Mr Kinnock began to glance down repeatedly at his prepared speech, and, as if to divert attention from his hesitant memory, his bodily gestures became increasingly lively and random. The finger pointed, the neck twitched, the head butted and butted some more. The body swayed, the hands flapped, the brows creased and decreased. From the mouth there emerged now a shout, now a whisper, now an impassioned yell. This part of the speech was on the need for self-discipline.

". . .It will make us fit to govern." And so ended this, the most recent most important speech in Mr Kinnock's career. He sat down to resounding applause. Seismologists in the audience even noted two tiny claps from Mr Skinner.   *30 September 1987*

In which an Analogy is discovered in the Family Fawlty

IT IS often amusing to be in a room with two people who get on each other's nerves, and if that room happens to be the Chamber of the House of Commons then so much the better.

While the Prime Minister and the Leader of the Opposition jabber at each other across The Table, observers find their minds drawn back to the episode of Fawlty Towers in which that excellent actress, Joan Sanderson, playing the part of The Deaf Lady, becomes increasingly irritated by the prognostications and gesticulated excuses of an exasperated Mr Basil Fawlty. "I want service!!!" she would yell, banging the reception bell ever more vigorously. Finding none, her conclusion would always be the same: "Silly man!"

During Prime Minister's Question Time, Mrs Thatcher never seems satisfied with the quality of the questions offered by the Proprietor of the National Conscience, Mr Neil Fawlty, sending them back time and time again. Certainly, Neil Fawlty is no champion of the nouvelle cuisine style of question, eschewing neat little fresh portions, exquisitely presented, in favour of well-boiled mushy servings, topped off with lashings of weak sauce, often identifiable as the warmed-up leftovers of the week before.

Mr Fawlty's first offering, which he slammed down on the table with some ferocity, concerned the nurses. Would she meet them? The Deaf Lady was having none of it: this was not what she had ordered, and he should go back to the kitchen and try again. Mr Moore was meeting the nurses, and that was quite enough.

"YOU! YOU! YOU!" blurted Mr Fawlty's loyal but haphazard staff, waving their arms frantically.

"I am delighted that people always want to see ME" declared The Deaf Lady, attempting to squidge the silly little man with her superior irony. Mr Fawlty's backroom staff began yelling incomprehensible slogans, foreigners all.

"Absolutely delighted!" shrilled The Deaf Lady above the hubbub.

Having had his first dish sent back so swiftly, Mr Fawlty disappeared back into the kitchen, swiftly re-appearing with another. "Why does she treat the nurses with such contempt? Why does she slam the door in their face?" Alas, The Deaf Lady was not slow to realize that, far from being offered an exciting new dish, she was being palmed off with the same dish under a different name. She was having none of it. She recited her own list of triumphs and resumed her perpetual complaints of the time in the late 1970s when she was forced to stay in an hotel run by Mr Fawlty's company. The service had been quite appalling.

At times like these, Mr Fawlty looks to his right and his left, a broad smirk playing on his face. His expression seems to suggest that the Lady is so barmy that there is no need to even bother to argue with her. Nevertheless, he recognizes that the Proprietor of the National Conscience has one or two duties he is obliged to perform, and so, with a sigh, he rises once more.

"If she has such faith in her figures, why does she not have the nurses into Number Ten to offer that recitation to them face to face? Why is she frightened to meet them?"

Recognizing a slightly new sauce to the dish, The Deaf Lady took a stab at it. Finding it not to her taste, she paraded it on a fork in front of all her fellow guests. "Which figures is the Rt Hon Gentleman challenging?" she screeched. "UP! UP! UP!" her fellow guests yelled at Mr Fawlty to answer. "RIGHT! RIGHT!" screeched The Deaf Lady. Mr Fawlty looked as if sick to death of the common riff-raff he was forever expected to entertain. "If he does not believe any figures given on this side of the House", continued the Deaf Lady, "why does he ask any questions?" And with that, she banged on the bell for a new question from someone other than this silly little man.

Hey presto, from out of the kitchen came a Conservative waiter, bowing and scraping. Was the Deaf Lady aware that the House would welcome the replies she gave on television last night. . .? The lady smiled. Now this was more like it: at last, someone who spoke her language.   *27 January 1988*

Concerning the Fraught communion between a Mother and her wayward Son

TOM AND Jerry, Andy and Flo, Basil and Sybil, even, no doubt, Napoleon and Josephine: the analogy hunters have explored a whole world of absurdity in their desire to express the bizarre relationship that exists between Mrs Margaret Thatcher and Mr Neil Kinnock. Ant and Bee, Man and Mouse, Victoria and Albert – and so it goes on.

But their relationship seems recently to have embarked upon a new phase, for which a true analogy can be found only in that most fundamental of all human relationships, the sweet but sometimes strained connection that links a mother to her son.

In the past, the Prime Minister has had little time for Mr Kinnock; if the family metaphor were to be maintained, Mr Kinnock would be cast as the pet mouse brought into the House by the unwelcome cousin. If she noticed him at all, Mrs Thatcher would simply slap at him with her broom. But now she seems to be warming to him. She scolds him, yes, but only because she is so eager for him to learn. In turn, he seems ever anxious to please her, forever sporting his new-found knowledge of the capitalist economy.

At Question Time, the Boy Kinnock rose and recited the lessons he had learnt. "Interest rates need to go lower", he said. Seeing that Mother looked interested, the Boy Kinnock said he thought "one can and indeed one must buck the market".

Mother Thatcher responded by praising the Chancellor's "most excellent speech on Tuesday", but said that it would have been "even better if it had been heard in quietness". This was believed to have been an admonishment towards the Boy's scruffy friends. How would the Boy ever take over the shop with friends like that?

But the Boy was keen to make amends and prove himself. "The country will be glad to note that Number 10 and Number 11 are one big happy family again", he said. He then recited his second lesson in economics, referring to managed floats. "But the Chancellor is a manager while she remains a floater", he declared, showing off his new words.

"Why doesn't he include the whole Cabinet in the happy family?" asked Mother, and the Boy Kinnock could be seen to laugh. In the old days, he would never laugh at her jokes, but now he accepts them like sweets. "She should discuss the matter further with Mr Kenneth Baker", he riposted, and they both smiled.

But the time had come for the Boy to recite his third lesson. This time, Mother seemed exasperated. He had been doing so well, but now it was back to square one. Mother huffed and puffed her annoyance. "Of course the Right Honourable Gentleman couldn't understand the significance of the last Budget in as far as he was listening. . .he doesn't understand because he

doesn't listen. . .I don't expect him to understand."

The Boy sat down, struggling hard to smile. A few cheery uncles put their heads around the door, trying to jolly up the atmosphere a bit.

Uncle Norman Tebbit praised the Chancellor, the economy, the Government, the lot. Mother's sniffles seemed to disappear. Uncle Norman had put it "in his own inimitable way and no one could have put it better". Someone else told her that the Budget was to be "greatly welcomed".

"It contains something for everyone", agreed Mother, smiling through her tears. But out of the corner of her eye, she saw the Boy nudging his rough friends in that coarse way of his. The young today are so very, very ungrateful.   *18 March 1988*

∞∞

Awakening Memories of Queen Victoria and General Tom Thumb

THE PRIME Minister proclaimed that London had, in real terms, gained "increased moneys" for its Health Service. In this, as in an increasing amount of other respects, she grows more like Queen Victoria every day. Queen Victoria, it will be remembered, used to employ the words "news" strictly in the plural, declaring, for instance, that "The news from Crimea are appalling". Mrs Thatcher now speaks along similar lines.

Occasionally, she will pronounce a word peculiarly, and Tory back-benchers are then forced into a decision over whether to follow her into this pronunciation and risk ridicule from the opposite benches, or to go their own way and face a lifetime of political isolation. A month or two ago, she spoke of a visit to CopenHARgen, and even the most sycophantic of her back-benchers found themselves stumbling over an exact repetition, preferring to sit in silence until they could congratulate her on her recent visit to Kent or York or somewhere more straightforward. From the more vulgar press gallery, though, could be heard faint choruses of Tommy Steele's winning showstopper, "Wonderful, wonderful, CopenHARgen."

Like Queen Victoria, she is learning to favour words draped in daintiness. During Question Time, she replied to Mrs Rosie Barnes by saying that she agreed with the formula the Honourable Lady had "enunciated". This left observers with the impression that Mrs Barnes had just passed a demanding examination in elocution, and was now receiving praise from a past master.

Question Time began, as usual, with the Prime Minister listing her engagements for the day. In the morning, she had attended the launch of the Tidy Britain campaign, most suitable trappings, her party seemed to feel, for the Regal Presence. Behind her came an appreciative smile from her red-faced ghillie, Mr Nicholas Fairbairn, clad in a chain-laden suit of his own design. Elsewhere on her benches, her subjects prepared themselves for a major clean-up of the members opposite.

Her subjects have keenly followed the Prime Minister's lead in believing that, when they open their mouths, they speak for nothing so puny as themselves, but for every decent, fair-minded citizen the length and breadth of the country. Mr Allan Stewart, the Conservative MP for Eastwood, spoke on behalf of "all ordinary Trades Unionists in Scotland" who were, he said, "appalled by what has happened" at the negotiations for the Ford plant in Dundee.

Queen Margaret applauded the "great effort" of the Engineering Union to come into the 20th century while thoroughly disapproving of the "sectional interests" of the others. Many of her Parliamentary speeches are now rather closer to Christmas broadcasts, in which the people are urged to do their very best, and she speaks glowingly of the great common purpose of all mankind. It is only when the great common purpose is revealed to be continued support for the Conservative Government that the natives grow restless.

Perhaps remembering General Tom Thumb's successful visit to Queen Victoria at Windsor, the Tory back-benchers urged Mr Neil Kinnock to address words to the Royal Presence. "UP! UP! UP!" they went, but General Tom Thumb was not to be moved. Instead he pursed his lips, posing stern-faced, as if for a commemorative statuette.

Other questioners came and went and finally the General deigned to rise. "WAAAGH! DUNDEE! DUNDEE! WAAAGH!" boomed the Tory regimental guard. General Tom Thumb wished to ask Her Majesty whether she agreed with the economic diagnoses of Lord Young or those of the Chancellor?

To ask a direct question of the ruling monarch is a well-known breach of etiquette, and Queen Margaret dismissed such presumption by ignoring it. "The Economy is being su-purrrr-latively handled," she retorted. She added that she was "not prepared to take lectures" from someone who had worked in a government that had presided over Britain's economic decline. Or questions, either, it seemed. For she gave no answer.   *23 March 1988*

During which Mr Kinnock ceases to Smile

A TENDENCY to smile can hamper a man's prospects, particularly if that man is Mr Neil Kinnock. He carries with him the burden of a natural light-heartedness. This would be commendable in either the back or the front half of a pantomime horse, or perhaps even in a more senior figure, such as Mother Goose, but it sits a little awkwardly on the shoulders of the Leader of the Opposition.

Just before Prime Minister's Questions, Mr Kinnock entered, as usual, with a swagger. While Mr Kenneth Baker was droning on about educational reform, Mr Kinnock nudged Mr Jack Straw, made a merry quip into his ear, leant over to repeat the quip to Mr Frank Dobson, chuckled, remembered where he was and forced the tips of his lips downwards to present what he takes to be a suitably statesmanlike facade.

Mr Kinnock's questions to the Prime Minister are often phrased like jokes. "I say, I say, I say – have you heard the one about. . .?" he will begin and, instead of the more traditional Englishman, Irishman and Scotsman, he will pop in one or another victim of some monstrous government plot. Alas, it is written into parliamentary procedure that, however humourless the incumbent prime minister, he or she is always allowed the last laugh.

Mr Kinnock wanted to know what she thought about the latest leaked document: was it a threat to national security, or was it proof of organized mendacity? Referring to it as a "received stolen document", Mrs Thatcher said that "so long as people are willing to receive them, there will be people willing to give them". Others in Mr Kinnock's position might have taken the opportunity to look affronted, disturbed, vehement, etc, etc, but Mr Kinnock chose to roar with laughter, grinning from left to right, rubbing his thighs and waving the document merrily.

After these guffaws Mr Kinnock generally betrays guilt feelings, as if a voice from Heaven has made him suddenly aware of the gravity of his position. He juts out his chin, folds his arms, stops nudging his neighbours and does his very best to look serious.

Of course, there are times when propriety forbids a smile. These include the duration of any speech by Mr Ron Brown, particularly if that speech is by way of being an apology. Mr Brown is everything Mr Kinnock would prefer him not to be. Loopy, impassioned, unrepentant, he sits in the new, polite, businesslike Labour Party like a beetle on a blancmange. While the beetle might find this the most comfortable of environments, the chef can betray signs of unease.

The Speaker announced that Mr Brown wished to make a personal statement. Mr Brown, expected to apologize, began to talk about the media instead. "The Hon Gentleman must make the statement agreed with me," said the Speaker. "We agreed many things. . ." began Mr Brown. By this time, there was uproar on the Tory benches, with the naughtier lads on the

Labour benches laughing their heads off. "If he doesn't wish to make the agreed statement, that puts a different complexion on it," said the Speaker. "Since you asked me to make a grovelling statement, I'm not going to read it out," said Mr Brown.

And so it went on. Everyone had some sort of expression on their face: Tories furious, Labour spokesmen embarrassed, Labour rebels amused, Labour whips pugnacious, Mrs Thatcher exasperated, and so on. Everyone, that is, except for Mr Kinnock, who looked straight ahead as if nothing were happening, the last sunbather on the beach after the tidal wave warning has sounded.

After Mr Brown had slouched out of the Chamber, aided by a hefty and aggressive shove from the Labour Deputy Chief Whip, who else but Mr Eric Heffer sprang to his defence, arguing that a personal statement should not have to gain prior approval from the Speaker. "Perhaps I've been living in a fool's paradise," he said, quite seriously. Mr Kinnock's straight face began to twitch at the ends, his lips fighting a battle to retain their composure. But in seconds, the battle was lost. Mr Kinnock let himself go and laughed, and laughed, and laughed.   *20 April 1988*

><><><><><><><><><><><><><><><><><><><><><><><><><><><><><><><><><><><><><><

Containing an Interesting dialogue on Things Christian

MRS THATCHER might have merited the odd mention in the pages of P G Wodehouse, or perhaps her very own chapter in E F Benson, but it is hard to see her squeezing into the pages of the New Testament with any great ease. Nevertheless, these were the surroundings she seemed to choose for herself in her speech to the synod of the Church of Scotland at the weekend.

Tory backbenchers seemed cock-a-hoop at her elevation, and wished to shower her with glad tidings of mass approval from their constituencies. For them, the four gospels are primarily concerned with Individual Responsibility and Getting On With It Yourself. When was it I saw you hungry? they would ask; and, not waiting for a reply, they would offer their own reply: "Oh, yes, I remember – when you weren't exercising your Individual Responsibility."

Looking back to the Old Testament, their new privatized, assertive, streamlined, economic version of the Five Commandments would most certainly include "Thou Shalt Not Whimper", "Shoplifters will be Prosecuted", "Don't Come Running to Me" and "Never Knowingly Undersold". The Jesus Christ of Tory backbench dreams was a first-class salesman for Free Enterprise, a sort of bearded Terence Conran.

Mr Roger Sims, the Conservative member for Chislehurst, wished to alert the Prime Minister to the widespread support for her speech to the synod, and wondered if she would care to reassert her principles of "Christian ethics and individual responsibility". The mutters and mumbles of the unbelievers began to ring around the Chamber. The two main parties are as divided on Christianity as they are on everything else: for the Labour Party, the Feeding of the Five Thousand represents a clear demand for the nationalization of the loaves and fishes industries while for the Conservatives it is a firm indication of market forces supplying the consumer with what he wants, when he wants it.

Mrs Thatcher thanked Mr Sims for his kind words. She reminded him that her speech was "an expression of personal beliefs and views". As a plague of complaining locusts prepared to flutter upwards from the benches opposite, she attempted to soothe the multitude by adding "others may disagree, but it is a mark of Christian manners and courtesy that we do so in a mannerly way". So now Jesus Christ, the Conservative member for Nazareth South, was not merely a go-getting entrepreneur but also a first class graduate from a leading school of etiquette.

Up popped Mr Neil Kinnock, ever the Doubting Thomas. Calling to mind recent cuts in child benefit and the end to free school meals, he wished to know which passage in the Bible most influenced the Hon Lady. Was it Pilate washing his hands? From a quick burst as the Archangel Gabriel, Mrs Thatcher was back to her less demanding role of Sybil Fawlty, indignant, furious, and always in the right. "He debases everything I believe in, trying to exchange quotations from the Bible across the Dispatch Box" she said, adding: "I made it perfectly clear in that speech that one simply cannot delegate the exercise of mercy and generosity to others". Far better, she seemed to imply, that mercy and generosity should be formed into a privatized company, Merc-Gen plc, so that all charitable acts could be scrutinized for efficiency and profitability before taking their position in the market place.

By this time, both sides of the House were screaming at each other, every member now a theologian, now an all-in wrestler. Even the normally demure Dame Jill Knight was bouncing up and down, pointing and yelling, moving this way and that, resembling from a distance nothing so much as a fist-fight in a rhododendron bush. When Mr Bill Walker, the last Tory in Scotland, said that his people were delighted by the speech, and that it was "a nice change to have a leader who's a practising Christian", Mr Edward Heath looked a little disgruntled, and half-motioned to complain, the original warder turned to whiner.   *25 May 1988*

In which the Sketchwriter visits the Kensington by-election to hear Mr Kinnock sing

MR NEIL Kinnock was sitting with his hands clasped, as if in prayer. He was listening to Mrs Ann Holmes, the Labour candidate for Kensington, as she spoke about the fortieth anniversary of the National Health Service in a deep, rather posh voice and friendly manner peculiarly reminiscent of Shirley Williams.

Mr Kinnock had forsaken the Palace of Westminster for a schoolroom in the back streets of Notting Hill, perhaps lured by the temptation of once again sitting next to someone who is not embarrassed to describe themselves as a Kinnockite. His own speech was rather more awkward than Mrs Holmes's, scribbled on sheets of House of Commons writing paper, a strange amalgam of the long-winded and the yobbish. Listening to Mr Kinnock switch from the one to the other carries with it the same shock that might be provided by Sir Harold Acton suddenly launching into an after-dinner medley of rugby songs.

He was, he announced, launching a new Labour Party campaign for an extra 40,000 blood donors, attempting to draw blood from "people of all politics and no politics". This was welcome news to people of just a little bit of politics. He rambled on about the terrible state the health service now found itself in, using long, serious words like 'peremptorily', while the eyes of the assembled journalists slowly glazed over. But, after exercising his synonyms, Mr Kinnock likes to nosedive straight into yobspeak. "We've had him on the ropes and now he's on the ropes again," he said of Mr John Moore, the Secretary of State for Social Services. "He'll be spreadeagled on the wire in the Chamber this afternoon." It was as if, halfway through his speech, Mr Kinnock had swapped his Roget's *Thesaurus* for the collected thoughts of Nobby Stiles.

If everything was so awful, asked one journalist, why were the Conservatives ahead in the polls? "Loadsamoney," said Mr Kinnock in a wacky Cockney accent, as if no one had imitated the expression before. "This Government has been spending money as if it's gone out of fashion," he said, "and among a proportion of the population there's a feelgood feeling." The yob was now well away, leaving all those 'peremptorily's' wiggling on their backs. Asked what was damaging Labour in the polls, he blamed "disputation in the party", adding: "The Unholy Alliance rules not OK."

But, once he is out among the people, Mr Kinnock seems on much more solid ground, particularly if those people are still attending nursery school. The cavalcade moved on to the Maxilla Nursery School. Mrs Holmes pointed at all the cameramen. "Loadsapictures," she explained to the children, her previous poshness now corrupted by her proximity to power. Suddenly, and for no obvious reason, she took to the piano, playing an old rock 'n' roll number while her leader sang. "Ohhh, plee-ease, way-ay-ait for me, Di-ana," he sang, and the children looked on askance, their troubled expressions making it clear they would prefer some more considered statement of current Labour Party policy.

"Have we got any stickers for the children?" asked a teacher. "Loadsastickers," replied Mr Kinnock, before moving outdoors to the slide in the garden. "Kinnock On The Slide" rehearsed one grouchy headline writer under his breath. Within seconds, a little girl in pink had begun to wail her head off. Other politicians would have zoomed away, anxious not to be pictured with any child not bearing a card-carrying grin, but Mr Kinnock leant over and picked her up, muttering comforting words ("Wassamatter? Wassamatter?") until she had calmed down. "So these cameras have the same effect on you as well, do they?" he joked.

Should Mr Tony Benn's present ambitions be fulfilled, Mr Kinnock might well consider taking up a new job working with children, or at least younger children. "What a face!" he says, feeding a mewling infant a sweetie. Mrs Thatcher is less adept with kiddies, demanding to know their names in a severe manner similar to that of the deputy headmistress in the excellent *Four Marys* comic strip. But then she has loadsapolicies to make up for it.   *6 July 1988*

The Conservatives held Kensington with a decreased majority

∞∞∞

In which the Prime Minister raises her Voice to complain about Noise

MY DEAR, the *noise* and the *people*! Mother Thatcher, Britain's most famous Cistercian, was finding it all a trifle rowdy. Again and again, she complained about the noisiness of the Chamber of the House of Commons. How odd, then, that only yesterday she should have picked Mr Eric Forth from the backbenches to turn him into a junior minister.

Mr Forth is quite the noisiest person in the Palace of Westminster, his mildest whisper drowning out any low-flying jets overhead. Meanwhile, Mr John Moore, whose quiet little croak of a voice has been lulling the House to sleep over the past year, has been demoted. The Noise Abatement Society has been poorly served by this Government, so it ill becomes Mrs Thatcher to shout her head off about noisiness.

But the Conservatives as a whole seem to take a peculiar view of their own Noise Creation Schemes. Whenever the Leader of the Opposition stands up, they cackle and heckle to their hearts' content. Yet the gentlest pin-drop from the Labour Party finds these very same Conservatives placing their hands over their ears while mouthing anxious complaints to the Speaker.

Having waited in that statesmanlike way of his (chin forward, eyes looking ever upward) for the welcoming row to die down, Mr Kinnock chose to use the brand new cabinet reshuffle for a brand old question: did the appointment of a new Secretary of State for Health mean that the Government would be providing the nurses' pay award in full?

It seemed many moons since the health crisis had been placed on the turntable. Just as some Government records top the crisis charts – unemployment, poll tax, privatization – they are just as surely bound to sink before long into happy oblivion. Play it again, Margaret, Mr Kinnock seemed to be saying, play it one more time – just for me. And so she did.

"I need not remind the honourable gentleman of the cuts to nurses' pay under the last Labour Government", she trilled, and Mr Kinnock appeared to be delightedly shaking his foot in time. It was like a delightful reunion of an Old Tyme Band: if only the late Mr Moore had been there, gargling his heart out before an appreciative audience, the nostalgic picture would have been complete. But soon this joyous trip down memory lane was curtailed by a brash Conservative member singing solo.

Mr Richard Alexander, whose career until now has been so hushed as to preclude all attention, rose to complain about the noise he found everywhere, particularly "some of the noise coming from car windows and from transistor radios". He found it all "deeply offensive" and – surprise! – called for urgent legislation.

"If I can be heard through the noise which is such a *terrible* example for schoolchildren", she replied later, unfairly blaming politicians for influencing the schoolchildren, when it is quite obvious that it is the schoolchildren who are influencing the politicians.

A Labour backbencher then had the novel idea of complaining about silence. He had somehow detected "widespread anger" in the country over the reward recently given to Mr Brittan for his silence over Westland. One of the distinguishing features between politicians and normal human beings is their skill at detecting widespread anger. Surveying the country, normal human beings are ill-equipped to discover much beyond widespread indifference. Mrs Thatcher's tribute to Mr Brittan's "excellence" brought forth much noise. "They can't debate – they can only shout!" she bellowed at the top of her voice.   *27 July 1988*

[49]

5
THE CONFERENCES

A broadly-based chapter Notable for the Realistic Approach it adopts to the Tackling of Important Issues and the Seeking of Fundamental Agreement, containing as many Resolutions and Amendments as a man could Want.

The Trades Union Conference
Containing metaphors drawn from the worlds of the Theatre, Natural History, and Children's Entertainment, all serving to throw a Vivid light on the Large figure of Mr Willis

THE LORD Mayor of Blackpool would normally be a figure out of Gilbert and Sullivan, or at very least Stanley Holloway, but this year he seems to have trundled out of Bertolt Brecht. "This woman and her friends" he said in his welcoming address, enunciating the word "friends" with a venom more usually employed by Mr Punch while walloping Judy, "this woman and her friends have got all the power and you'll not get it off them by nibbling".

Will the Lord Mayor of Blackpool be asked to give a similar address to the Conservative Conference early next month? Will he even now be genning up politely on the particular irritations of the Tories? Will that woman become that man? As his chain of office sends glints and gleams on to his unmemorable face, will he rant against Mr Kinnock and his friends, if any?

It will be hard for him to find such a crowd-pleaser as Mrs Thatcher. The mere mention of her name is on a level with the Tolpuddle Martyrs and This Great Movement of Ours and Our Brothers in South Africa in its effect of ensuring a feeling of cosiness among all comrades. At least we are agreed on that one, you can hear them murmur appreciatively.

So delighted was Mr Norman Willis with the Lord Mayor's welcome that he presented him with a copy of a hardback edition of the *History of Trades Unionism*, a very good joke indeed. But even after ten minutes of the first morning of the 119th Trades Union Congress, the warmth was still not yet quite exhausted. On the platform were fellow Trades Unionists from Canada, Denmark, South Africa, the USA and goodness knows where. You could tell they were strangers. They were smiling. The head of the American Trades Unions gave a speech saying that both organizations were speaking the same language, "the language of safety and dignity on the job". Had he been informed, wrongly, that he was addressing the British Medical Association?

There were two elements to the first day's proceedings. The first was the new, with-it image of Trade Unionism. The second was the debate over no-strike agreements. The two elements went together as delightfully as congealed milk on a fresh cup of coffee. Spearheading the new, with-it image was Mr Norman Willis, who, with his slobbering mouth, vast bald head and giant wing-span, argued forcefully that the TUC was not the dinosaur the media were intent on portraying it to be.

Mr Willis was delighted to introduce two or three short films commissioned by the General Council to prove that the TUC is an organization for today's world. With-it as he is, Mr Willis does not favour new-fangled media-influenced devices such as being able to read his own writing. "The short film you are about – " he said, turning over the page, and at that point he lost his place. Seconds later, the words " – to see" emerged.

The hall went dark, and on to the screen came the gorgeous nostalgia of the voice of a veteran from Pathe News coupled with a succession of people – young and old, behatted and hatless, smiling and smiling harder. Were these all enthusiastic chewers of Wrigley's Spearmint Gum? No – they were happy Trades Unionists, though we had to take this on trust, for they bore as much resemblance to the increasingly grumpy delegates in the hall as chirruping sparrows to a sackful of cats.

After lunch, Mr Willis once again spoke the new language of Trades Unionism. "Watching us on television now – or not watching us because they are at work – are thousands of people whose jobs have been saved by the Trades Union movement". "Many harsh things have been said and done. Frankly, many of them would have been better not said and not done". "What would any newspaper have – what would anyone give to have – nine people – nine million people – reading them?" How the Lord Mayor of Blackpool, now snug in his bed, must be longing to read the next chapter in the *History of Trades Unionism*, modern, slick and punchy.

8 September 1987

<hr />

In which Mr Jarvis counts to Five Hundred

"THREE seven three, three seven four, three seven five. . ." Mr Fred Jarvis spent most of his day counting to five hundred. ". . .Three seven six, three seven seven, three seven eight, three seven nine. . ." His experience in the teaching profession was coming to the fore. ". . .Three eighty, three eight one, three eight two. . ."

He has been too lenient with his class over the past three days, allowing them to speak way after the five-minute bell has gone. This means that there is a tremendous backlog of debates to get through. As most debates are not debates at all but communal sing-songs against the wrongs of the world, it is easier for Mr Jarvis to simply read out the hymn numbers rather than go to the effort of hearing them sung. ". . .Three eight three, three eight four, three eight five. . ." as he read out each number, he allowed a decent length of time – say, a billionth of a second – for anyone to leap up and say yes, they liked what was happening to the NHS, yes, they were behind Mrs Thatcher all the way in her out-and-out attack on the very foundations stones of democracy and yes, they couldn't be happier with a full-scale nuclear war as soon as one could possibly be arranged.

". . .Three eight six, three eight seven, three eight eight. . ." If only he had thought of this method on the first day, everyone could have been away from Blackpool before the first chip had hit the pan.

Debate by number makes poor television and, sensing this, head office at TV-am had dispatched their TUC crew to Manchester, where the oldest cat in Britain was celebrating her birthday with a smattering of her 312 kittens. But seasoned observers know that a lull in the congress means that Mr Arthur Scargill is extracting snooker cues from his neck ready to look his best for the storm. Had Mr Jarvis been able to whisper a number rather than announce Mr Scargill's amendment to the general council's report on nuclear energy, he would have done. But Mr Scargill had earlier proved himself no unilateralist when it came to man-to-man combat, so Mr Jarvis introduced his own barrage balloon, in the shape of Mr Norman Willis.

In his weirdly childish voice, wearing what looked uncommonly like an Old Etonian tie, Mr Willis attempted to win Mr Scargill round on human-itarian grounds. The council had been all around the world from the Orkneys to the Ukraine, meeting 15 times, including two weekend sessions, asking all sorts of questions of all sorts of people and had still found time to draft a report.

Though unlike Scheherezade in most other respects – he has little or no Arabian blood in him, for instance – Mr Norman Willis is a dab hand at employing the ever-continuing story to stave off impending congressional death. The report, he told bloodthirsty sultans Jordan and Scargill, was not yet over, and it was well worth waiting until next year for the punchline. "Our work is not complete. . .These motions jump the gun when there are important hurdles left to jump", he said, speaking in a free translation from the original English.

Bill Jordan was won over by the allure of such narrative mystique, dropping his amendment, but Arthur, as always, took his cue. "This is an issue that has concentrated the minds of most people for 30 years", he blared, perhaps over-pessimistically, "and a decision cannot be delayed for another 12 months!" Poor Norman looked downcast and began playing with his pen. But Arthur was not yet finished. He had some figures at his fidgety fingertips. If 40,000 deaths were going to arise from Chernobyl, a good 400,000 would arise from a similar accident in Britain.

"TIME! TIME! TIME!" screamed the delegates. The little red light had come on and Arthur's story had to end. But minutes later he was back for the summing up. "Just four points. . ." he began, as likely an introduction as Mr Tommy Cooper's "But seriously. . ." After roughly a thousand points, he returned to his seat, whereupon his amendment was thrown out, and the debates were back to normal. ". . .Three ninety, three nine one, three nine two. . ."

11 September 1987

The Liberal Party Assembly
Containing a riddle, a rabbit and a Bogus Major

"I FOR one", they all say at some stage during their speeches: I for one think this, I for one think that.

Mr Cyril Smith spoke early in the day. "I for one", he said – and observers were tempted to demand a recount – "I for one consider David Steel handled himself very well in a very difficult situation."

David Steel! We had almost forgotten about him. Liberals have a remarkably short shelf-life. Left for more than a week or two, they either go right off or disappear. Senior Labour and Conservative MPs need only put their heads around the door of the House of Commons once in a blue moon and they still remain famous, but if a Liberal so much as nips out for a breath of fresh air, before he reappears people start wondering which one he was, what he is doing now, and whether he is dead. Perhaps to compensate for the speed with which they dematerialize, the Liberals speak in ever grander phrases. After "I for one" come the words "dream", "vision", "the 21st century", "regeneration" and "principles", in no particular order, and often all at the same time.

"Have courage! Dream dreams! Have vision!" said Mr Smith. For a moment it seemed that he was about to burst into a rousing medley of the greatest hits of Peter, Paul and Mary, but instead he waddled back to his seat, stretched his small hands across the vast globe of his belly, smiling open-mouthed at the applause he was receiving.

Though the day in the conference hall lasted eight hours and saw 55 speakers, there was only one speech, and that repeated every five minutes. It began with regrets for the results of the last election, continued with a plea not to give up hope, asked everyone to give the new party a go and concluded with something along the lines of: "Let us look beyond the present to the future, beyond the future to the past and into the present by way of the future", followed by long and sympathetic applause.

"What an adventure! What a challenge! Let's take it!" were Mr Des Wilson's concluding words. His face is Famous Five out of Brer Rabbit, his words roughly the same. It is hard to think of sitting in a committee room for three months with Mr Bob Maclennan in quite such enthusiastic terms, but everyone at the Liberal Assembly is Bob mad.

What do you call a man with no arms and no legs swimming in a sea of Liberalism? The answer, of course, is Bob. He appeared onstage halfway through the afternoon, as pristine as a shaved peach, vaguely reminiscent of a junior member of the Royal Family, a retired princess maybe, or even a defrocked viscount. But in real life he is leader of the SDP, a man dedicated to thrashing things out around tables and other such adventures and challenges.

Throughout the day he had the opportunity to observe his future colleagues. Mr Richard Holme, looking more than ever like a bogus major specializing in defrauding spinsters in forgotten seaside towns, spoke of the good times they'd have together. Mr Alan Beith spoke of being entrusted with the freedom of future generations. Mr Simon Hughes spoke of the Earth and its fruits.

With so much goodwill pouring out towards mankind, young and old, male and female, rich and poor, Bob could feel excused for feeling slightly nauseous. "It has been a very hard road to hoe", said Mr David Alton, exposing his inner-city origins, before quoting Martin Luther King, second only to The Tolpuddle Martyrs in this year's name-dropper's Conference Manual.

Next came Michael Meadowcroft. "We need have no inferiority complex", he said, though looking at him, skilled observers found it hard to think why on earth not. In the auditorium, people shuffled to and fro, saying thank you and sorry as they bumped elbows and knees. "I for one" said the next speaker, and everyone sat comfortably.   *16 September 1987*

∞∞

In which the Sketchwriter demonstrates the Full Breadth of his Reading

MURDER ON THE HARROGATE EXPRESS
On December 17, 1926, Agatha Christie was discovered living under a pseudonym in the Old Swan Hotel, Harrogate. More than 60 years later, uncanny occurrences at Harrogate suggest that her spirit still exerts an uneasy influence. For there has been a murder on the Harrogate Express. The body of forceful Dr Owen, once the most popular figure in the town, has been discovered in the driver's compartment. Multiple stab wounds disfigure his back. Yet he never made an enemy in his life. Or did he? Now read on. . .

FOR a moment or two Poirot remained lost in thought. "*C'est terrible, mon vieux*", he said. "*Mais*, there is always an *explication*."

The carriage stirred uncomfortably. Nice Mrs Williams from the corner-shop seemed to develop a twitch. She always had a cheery word for everyone, and wouldn't hurt a flea. Or would she? Underneath her fluffy pink slipper, Poirot noticed a flea lying dead, squashed without mercy.

[55]

Forgetful old hangdog William Rodgers, always losing his seat, shifted from one foot to another, an axe dangling any-old-how from his hand. Moustachioed Captain Holme played agitatedly with his blow-pipe. Young David Alton played nervously with the phial of arsenic he insisted was for his asthma. They seemed such a nice gang – but among them was a murderer!

Strange Mr Maclennan – always so well turned out – kept repeating, "I stand before you today as your Doctor", again and again under his breath. But why, thought Poirot. The village already had a doctor. And now he was dead.

"*Mon vieux*", said Poirot. 'A body we have. For sure that is. And if we have a body – we must also have a murderer – *mais non?*"

"He made wounding and ungrateful attacks on us all." The voice of Shirley Williams broke the chilly silence. "They were painful. Sad. And damaging."

"*Oh la la*", said Poirot. "He had his enemies, our Doctor Owen, *eh bien?*"

The train plunged into a tunnel.

"He is immensely unfortunate in the kind of people who admire him. Let us say no more." The kindly voice of David Steel crackled through the darkness. As daylight returned, Poirot noticed bloodstains on Steel's teeth.

In the distance, poor mad Greave ran round in circles. He and the Doctor had never got on. That was no secret. But was that a likely motive for hatred – even for murder?

"I stand before you today as your Doctor, I stand before you today as your Doctor, I stand before. . ."

"Shut up! For Pete's sake shut up!!" Fiery-haired Charles Kennedy finally snapped. He could take the manic burblings of Maclennan no more.

Might they have been accomplices in the dreadful deed, wondered Poirot to himself. But were they not the Doctor's *amis plus chers*? It all seemed so very unlikely.

Poirot turned to Des, the cheery red-faced butler whose appearance from New Zealand had never been fully explained. "*Eh bien, Monsieur,* you worked for *le médecin, mais non?*"

"I worked with the Doctor every day, m'lud", blurted Des. "He was as much a victim of the position as we were."

"Yet you are all alive and he is – 'ow you say? – dead." The word stilled the air.

"Tickets please! Tickets please!" Bluff Mr Smith swung his body into the carriage, causing the Harrogate Express to give a sudden lurch. From his vast pocket fell a club embedded with nails. "It's for me garden", he explained, putting it back in his pocket. "Ho, Ho". But his laughter seemed strangely hollow.

"*Mesdames et messieurs*" said Poirot confidently. "I have a solution to the affair of *le médecin mort*." A tremor of fearful expectation rushed through the carriage.

"He had a secret. A secret *tres terrible*. He knew power. He loved power. And you. . ." his piercing eyes circled the carriage, fixing its glare on

everyone. ". . .you hated him for it. *Eh bien* – you killed him. You are all guilty, all of you. *Voilà!*"

And so the Harrogate Express hurtled on through the night, its course steady for oblivion.   *19 September 1987*

∞∞∞

The Labour Party Conference
In which an Hotel brochure and an Official Statement are Wilfully muddled by the Tiresome sketchwriter

"WELCOME to your Great Escape Weekend. I hope that you will find it a most enjoyable one". Thus runs one of the many brochures offered by the brand new Ramada Renaissance Hotel in Brighton, whose Presidential Suite is the home of Mr and Mrs Neil Kinnock this week.

Guests leave the Ramada Renaissance Hotel laden with brochures inviting them to enjoy personal attention to their every whim. In the short walk to the Brighton Conference Centre, further literature is thrust upon them – for seals, against bombs, for esperanto, against smoking, for abortion, against the Contras. By and large, it is easy to distinguish hotel brochure from political pamphlet. Few five star international hotels with a reputation to maintain would invite their clientele to WAKE UP BEFORE IT IS TOO LATE! for instance. Nor would the words SMASH and WRECK be as recurrent in a brochure for, say, a new cocktail lounge, jacuzzi or solarium as they are in an invitation to join Militant. On entering the hall the difference between the two becomes less easily discernible.

Moving ahead is the title of the official Labour Statement to Conference. It is packaged in saloon-bar beige, a red rose sprouting from its black lettering, its head looking nervously to the right, like a flower searching anxiously for its home in a wreath. Inside, all is luxury. As in the Ramada message, the emphasis of the dishes offered is on freshness and natural flavours.

Moving ahead is consumer-oriented. Its concluding message, reprinted on the back: "Labour's commitment is to create as well trained a workforce as our European competitors within ten years", might as easily have been "The customer is always right". A crazed activist, running amok with kitchen scissors, might scramble the competing promises of hotel and party and, having done so, spend the rest of his life trying to reassemble them:

- Our success depends on putting forward our own policies in a way that is attractive and positive.
- At all times there is a cosmopolitan crowd engaged in lively conversation across the marble topped tables.
- We will be staging a number of "Labour Listens' events in the regions.
- We never forget that our guests are individuals.
- Our task is to show people that we are on their side – as individual citizens.
- Offering a vision of the future – a vision with wide appeal across the nation.
- Everything is designed to give guests the feeling that this is the lifestyle they would like to enjoy always.
- Democratic socialism is thus about extending the freedom of the individual – every individual, in every family, in every community and every part of the country.
- Its unique atmosphere delights everyone.

General Secretary Larry Whitty, a gentleman whose moustachioed features seem to be assembled from a democratic pooling of the "Meet the Team" placards in every seaside Odeon, welcomed guests to the new Labora Hotel. But he did not allow the destruction of the shabby Old Labora to pass without due mourning. First came the good news. "This summer, we gave new hope to the British people". Then the bad. "But the fact is we lost".

So saying, he prodded the lectern forcefully with his right forefinger, as if pressing the button that might finally send the casket through the swiftly shutting doors and into the flames. He then listed the potential guests who went elsewhere in the summer. The list stretched from the young to the old, taking in most of the middle-aged as well. Parents, children, young marrieds, old marrieds: it seemed to stop short only at the immediate family of Mr Neil Kinnock. "We couldn't convince people we could deliver or maintain their current security and comfort", Mr Whitty explained. And so management had moved elsewhere and – tarantara – welcome to the new Labora Renaissance Hotel.

But experts predict complaints from those block-booked into the new Labora. It may be beautiful and it may be modern. But it hasn't yet been built.   *29 September 1987*

In which Fingers are wagged and Threats are exchanged

"**I**S NEIL to be fixed by these guys?" In Parliament, Mr Tam Dalyell speaks like a man whose tongue has been dipped in the prose of *The Eton College Chronicle*, circa 1860. But in the less, shall we say, civilized environs of the Labour Party Conference he adopts a more streetwise lingo. It is just a shame that the street he chooses should be in Tombstone Gulch.

He was referring to those he described as "the so-called security services", but, were he to widen the circumference of his circle of conspiracies only slightly, he might also have included the other guys who were intent on fixing Neil – the Big Bad Unilateralist Gang. Tired of taking pot-shots at the Government, they were out to get the real two-timing Mr Big.

A delegate with horn-rimmed glasses and a small moustache kicked off the unilateralist debate. "When we win the next General Election – and we will. . ." he began, using the catchphrase that has cropped up every few minutes during this conference, ". . .we will be facing a very different world than we do today". On the platform, Mr Kinnock seemed to breathe easily, for this has been his favourite excuse for doodling on the party's clean white unilateralist pad.

But the man with the small moustache then unbuttoned the cloak of his gist to reveal a well-stocked shoulder-holster beneath. "Neil", he said – always a bad sign – "Neil, when you became leader and long before, you made statements affirming your commitment to unilateralism. I urge you to reaffirm that commitment."

Neil looked statesmanlike, his preferred posture when feeling sheepish. Time was running out for the man with the small moustache, so he quickly added: "I beg you not to abdicate the policy on which we won the election". As he returned to his seat, the rest of the delegates looked a trifle awkward. Who would be man enough to tell him the awful news?

Mr Eric Hammond, of course. Mr Hammond loves being man enough to deliver awful news; indeed, it is his prime enjoyment in life. Not for him the shilly-shally; were he a hospital visitor, he would bring comfort to the afflicted by dressing in black, lustily swinging his thurible and singing "Abide With Me" at the top of his voice. Following in the long tradition of the great movement, his appearance at the rostrum was greeted with boos and hisses.

Mr Hammond suggested controversially that they had lost the election. He then produced figures from a poll of his own union to suggest that his members wouldn't say no to a bomb or two. Wagging his finger in the air he said "You will not quickly be forgiven if you continue your error!"

The unnerving aspect of Mr Hammond is that, among delegates whose voices tend to start at a screech and escalate towards the ear-piercing, he remains dull and monotone throughout. "Make the choice between permanent protest and power!" The shrill outcries that greeted this suggested that, for most delegates, the choice was perfectly easy.

Throughout the hall, delegates stood, their hands outstretched in the direction of the chairman. On one side stood Mr Ken Livingstone, on the other Mr Arthur Scargill. The choice fell on Mr Scargill. "I say this to Conference", he screamed, "if there is any thought in the mind of the platform of abandoning our unilateralist commitment, it will be hypocrisy at its worst."

Just as Mr Livingstone had previously spoken of "civil war" in the party, Mr Scargill now spoke of "internecine warfare". For such peace-loving fellows, the imagery that prowls the dark corridors of their minds is curiously combative.

Up popped Mr Denis Healey bearing the suppressed grin he always displays whenever a street brawl is promised. Addressing the conference in the manner of a long-serving prep-school master who has better things to do than waste his time talking to a lot of wretched children, he said that there was no room in the debate for threats. He then rounded on Mr Livingstone, declaring forcefully that those who used the issue for personal political advantage would not be forgiven. To the untrained ear, this sounded curiously like a threat.   *2 October 1987*

<hr>

The Arrival of Spot, whose Tale is Told to Mr and Mrs Kinnock, who Express concern

OUTSIDE the Ramada Renaissance Hotel, a Theatrical Removals lorry stood waiting. On the seafront, a phalanx of photographers loitered beside an inflatable castle called *Bumpa Bouncer Supa Bounce*. Alongside it, a red ribbon was strung across the entrance to Brighton Council's first playbus, a converted double-decker christened *Fun One*, ready for snipping by the leader of the Labour Party.

The Kinnocks arrived 10 minutes late, Neil buttoning up his jacket button, Glenys beaming in a Liberty print. Within seconds, a baby apiece had been thrust in their arms. "Helloooo. Helloooo", cooed Glenys as her baby struggled for his freedom, yelling his demands not just for himself but for all babies everywhere. Meanwhile, Neil's baby's nose began to run.

"Let's have a successful nose-blowing exercise", said Neil, thinking that he could simply wipe away everything that had been built up without reference to grassroots opinion.

"What's this, hmmmm? What's this? Here's a silly thing", Glenys was pointing out a fur-muffed microphone to her baby. He was obviously still hopelessly ignorant of the machinery of the blatantly anti-babyist capitalist media.

"Great to have you here", said the chairman of the Brighton Parks and Recreation Committee, handing the scissors to the Labour leader. Showing deep commitment to all ribbon-snipping programmes, Mr Kinnock engineered a deep and severe cut in the ribbon to cheers from Labour activists. From behind the photographers emerged an 8ft cuddly bear. "This is terrifying", said Glenys.

"Turn this way a bit, turn this way", shouted the photographers, but even bears have their rights. The Labour Bears Against Media Harassment group would have a thing or two to say about this. Ms Patricia Hewitt then helped turn the bear round to face photographers, and he stood, waving, next to the Labour leader.

Neil looked unsure whether to smile at his baby or his bear. "God, we do some ridiculous things", he muttered. "Shall we go on the bus now?"

Inside the bus, two little children were armed with paint brushes loaded with bright red paint, living embodiments of the need for an emergency paint control resolution from conference. "TO NEIL", were the words under a painting of a red rose, splattered and shambolic, giving every indication that it had been run over by a steamroller.

One of the children embarked on a painting of a red circle with something dark in the middle. Quite possibly it was a free-form study of Mr Ken Livingstone. This might explain why Mr Kinnock seemed intent on covering it with green paint. "What's this? What's this?" he asked the child, smothering Ken in green, adding: "It's a bush. It's a bush".

"Tracey's going to paint herself here picking flowers", Neil explained to the photographers, pointing at an area dangerously close to where Mr Livingstone was lurking, covered in bush. "Adding too much water makes it too watery", Glenys advised Tracey. But as self-elected chair of the Tracey Defence Caucus, Neil forthwith issued the following statement: "Tracey wants white now".

Upstairs in the bus, pamphlets showed the Life of Spot. Spot can see you. That's a silly place to hide, Spot. Calm down, Spot. Spot is behind the door. For a time, the Labour leader made a deep and serious review of the comings and goings of Spot, but then he began to show signs of distress that the child delegates showed more interest in Spot than him. "They don't give a damn that we're here", he complained, managing a smile.

"Neil's winding it up", stated Ms Patricia Hewitt in a press statement.

"Great. Right", said Neil, waving goodbye to the children.

"Back to mummy then", said Glenys.

After his official visit to *Fun One*, Mr Kinnock gave an interview to the small press corps on the seafront. "How much of a change do you think it marks for the party?" went the first question. The process of winning back the diaper vote had just begun. *3 October 1987*

The Conservative Party Conference
The Opinions of Mr Moore concerning the British people, and other matters

T HE FIRST rule of the Tory Party conference is that any statement followed by an expectant pause from the speaker is vigorously applauded. Lose your place for more than three seconds and you earn a standing ovation. Instantaneous applause becomes so attractive that some speakers cannot will themselves away from the sycophantic statement into the main breach of their argument. Time is called before the complimentary slogans are drained. "Nurses, police and the armed forces are all there to help when you are in trouble", said Mrs Sheila O'Bairne, following through with a robust pause. Sure enough, a smattering of polite applause. "The winter of discontent must never happen again." Pause; applause. "And what is more. . ." said Sheila. "Could you wind up, Sheila", said the chairman. And so no one ever got to hear what Sheila originally intended to say.

The Joy of Unanimity is too pressing an urge for delegates to resist. But once they have attacked Arthur Scargill ("Hear! Hear!") and praised Mrs Thatcher ("Hear! Hear!"), they become so absorbed with not rocking the boat that they can only mouth truisms: "Without doubt – and I say this loudly and strongly – Tuesday in this great country of ours has always followed Monday. And let's keep it that way!" (Pause: Applause.)

But soon the main feature of the morning – The Man With No Face – was to appear. "Ladies and Gentlemen", announced the chairman, in a manner reminiscent of the Eurovision Song Contest, "please give a warm welcome to the Secretary of State for Social Services – The Rt Hon John Moore."

This curious man, his bland features never quite amounting to a complete face, acknowledged the applause with a mirthless smile. Within seconds, he forcefully declared that "the future of the basic state pensions is not open to question" and that the NHS "should not be used as a political football". He spoke of St Bartholomew's Hospital, opened in 1123 for the care of the poor. "Let me make this quite clear once and for all – there is no way in which this proud tradition is going to be abandoned".

Each vacant statement was followed by a quick furrow of the eyebrows and a purposeful stare into the middle distance, a combination designed to indicate resolve and integrity. Meanwhile, the intended suggestion that here might be a normal human being was jilted by Mr Moore's peculiar and recurrent habit of rolling his tongue around in his mouth whenever his lips were closed, as if he were forever scouring his teeth to ensure the shiny whiteness so favoured by the photogenic.

"I am prepared to accept that other parties care very much about the health service." As his speech bounded towards such heights of controversy,

Mr Moore's hands would make sudden but minute motions into the air.

Even when Mr Moore set his voice aquiver, presumably to indicate personal emotion, it emerged as more as an amateur yodel. "Throughout our history, the British people" – ah those British people – "have helped those less fortunate than themselves." His tongue went on its lengthy journey around the interior of his cheeks. He wished, he said, to make "real improvements in the life of our country."

Throughout this week, experts have stood in the Blackpool Winter Gardens, employed to listen to the Tory policy speeches and extract the meaning from the meandering. Most ministers have managed to insert at least a half sentence of policy somewhere in the midst of the Loony Leftery and This Great Country of Ours. But Mr Moore said nothing at all. He is the latest in a long line of favourites to succeed the Prime Minister. But if the Prime Minister retires and leaves a gap, the question will remain: Can a gap be filled by a gap? *9 October 1987*

The Conservative Women's Conference
Containing what the Reader may, perhaps, expect to find in it

IN THE mind of the Conservative Woman, the outside world is a horrifying thing indeed. There are the rising tides of pornography and mindless violence. There is the steady erosion of family values and traditional morality. Knives, guns, bad grammar and Mr Ken Livingstone abound. In many ways, being a Conservative Woman must be rather like being an eternal extra in a film directed by Mr John Carpenter.

The annual Conservative Women's Conference is thus a plush refugee camp in which comfort and succour are sought from their leaders. They are fuelled by a paranoia oddly similar to that of the hard left. "We have a hostile press which is always praising left-wing achievements," announced one speaker, and others saw obscenity and propaganda and degradation behind every bush and tree.

It seemed odd that the women should turn first to Mr Nicholas Ridley for reassurance on these matters. It is rather like applying to a python for a friendly lick or a bull for a pat on the back. In the House of Commons, Mr Ridley relishes his uncompromisingly uncharming image, snapping and grumbling in a manner curiously reminiscent of Mr Albert Steptoe. But at the Conservative Women's Conference he did his very best to be good, even pretending on occasion to take note of their points.

How he had changed! Where in the House of Commons, he would say, "stupid question", here he praised "many excellent speeches, bringing out all the different points of view". Where in the House of Commons he would goadingly smack his lips at the prospect of tarmacking a nice bit of Capability Brown, here he said: "No one wants to protect our green and pleasant land more than I." Exhausted at such niceness, Mr Ridley must have crawled back to the House of Commons a broken man, desperate for the cool, clear water of obscenity and mindless violence.

Mr Hurd had a more difficult task. He likes to talk of "creative solutions" and "imaginative thinking" in regard to the world of crime, whereas the women who preceded him were less *South Bank Show* in their diagnoses. "Criminals, thugs and louts do not respond to this trendy approach," said one. "In other words, we have to bring back the birch." This merited a warm round of applause. Mr Hurd screwed up his eyes and pretended to jot something down. His subsequent speech was littered with plain-talking, no-nonsense phrases such as "When I say punishment, I mean punishment", but, for all his tough-talking, he seemed to leave the conference hall with the uneasy impression that, in practice, he would fall short of reintroducing capital punishment for persistent bad language.

[65]

Before Mr John Moore took to the dais came the awful spectre of Mrs Teresa Gorman MP. "Who loves the menopause woman?" she said. "Who loves her when she gets those horrible hot flushes?" Her speech was intended to be in favour of Health Care for the over-50s. An accompanying brochure asked the question, "Can we grow old with grace and dignity like the Queen Mother. . .?" Even though Mrs Gorman said things like "I'm not ageing, I get younger every day" with as much grace and dignity as a superannuated go-go dancer, she still seemed to believe that the answer was "yes".

Mr Moore addressed the conference like a particularly flirtatious disc-jockey. "Teresa, wherever you are, I always get hot flushes when I see you," he purred, and all the ladies cooed and giggled. "I have to confess to being a mere male," he continued, before saying how glad he was that over the past few months he had managed to initiate such a far-ranging debate on health. Ho, ho.

Tarantara! After a slippery slick of Mr Kenneth Baker came "very much the moment you've all been waiting for". Jubilant smiles greeted the Prime Minister, who spoke to them as a housewife to housewives. "I can't help reflecting that it's taken a government headed by a housewife with experience of running a family to balance the books," she said. Oh, how happy she made them!   *26 May 1987*

6
QUESTION TIME

Being a Concise survey of the many Grave and Comic questions Posed by Members to Ministers, with one or two Replies

Defence Questions
In which Mr Nicholas Soames asks after the Whereabouts of Miss Atkin

IF MS SHARON Atkin can no longer command the support of the Labour Party, she can still count on Mr Nicholas Soames to keep her name alive. Sprucely dressed, with a pink handkerchief blossoming from his top pocket, Mr Soames yelled the name "Sharon Atkin"* with the enthusiasm and constancy with which his schoolmates would have yelled "Jennifer Eccles" all those years ago.

While earnest Labour backbenchers spoke *sotto voce* of the immense cost of Trident, Mr Soames yelled either "We want Sharon" or "What about Sharon?" At the close of each of these witticisms, he would rub his hands up and down his upper legs, guffawing to himself, using the full force of his body to turn his neck to ensure that his fellow Tories were similarly enjoying themselves.

There were times when the neighbour to his right seemed to be tiring of the joke. Sensing his hesitancy, Mr Soames would turn to the neighbour on his left, Mr Toby Jessel, to share in the merriment. By now, the Socialists had turned to the problem of jobs sacrificed on an altar of political ideology. Keeping his gibes needle-sharp, Mr Soames shouted "Sharon!" but, unaccountably, Socialists went on complaining.

As the defence debate continued, Mr Soames chose to make the peculiar gesture of drawing his clenched hands together as if forming a socket and then, forcing them suddenly apart, issuing the cry "Pwah!". What could this mean? Had Mr Soames gained an advance insight into a major new defence weapon? Was he taking a leaf from the book of Mr Campbell-Savours and spilling beans, only this time through the unimpeachable medium of mime? As his fellow Conservative, Mr Robert Atkin (presumably no relation) heckled, Mr Soames returned to the more conventional weaponry of a straight "Hear! Hear!"

Undeterred, Mr Denzil Davies began listing sums spent on defence. Slipping up, he said either six million when he should have said six billion, or vice versa. Alerted to this mistake by the chortles of his fellow Tories, Mr Soames shouted "Big Bang! Big Bang!", a trifle enigmatically, rounding it off with, "And he's the only one who can add!"

Mr Dale Campbell-Savours was soon to his feet mentioning a few of the remaining groups in the country who have yet to kill or be killed as part of a cover-up. "CS Gas! CS Gas!" shouted Mr Atkin. "CS Gas!" he shouted again, but his colleagues' stationary features indicated that much of the richness of this play on initials had been lost on them.

When his fellow O.E., Mr Tam Dalyell, rose to his feet, Mr Soames began holding out his fingers, as if inspecting a manicure. Mr Dalyell spoke of things sinister in a voice of such extreme bass that it was as if someone were playing a 45rpm record at 33rpm, randomly adjusting the volume switch at the same time.

Just as observers were beginning to suspect that Mr Soames had said his bit for the day, Mr Dennis Canavan happened to mention the name of Mr Caspar Weinburger. Mr Soames yelled, "Whingebag", though whether this was directed at the English or American politician is not recorded.

At the entry of the Prime Minister, Mr Soames chose to pull his pink hankie from his top pocket and took to shining his spectacles. "Quite right!" he heckled the minute the Prime Minister opened her mouth. He then returned his handkerchief to his pocket, puffing it up with care.

For the remainder of Prime Minister's Question Time, Mr Soames fidgeted wildly, crossing his arms, yawning a little, chatting a lot, now reviewing his ample cuffs, now experiencing what seemed like a little gum trouble. His only further contribution to the debate was to make what can only be described as a doggie noise when Mr Kinnock rose.

When the Prime Minister exited, so too did Mr Soames, leaving Labour talk of desperation, dissatisfaction and assassination far behind him.

6 May 1987

---

* Sharon Atkin had been dropped as a Labour candidate for expressing extreme views.

∞∞

Transport Questions
In which the Sketchwriter tackles the Question of the possible Madness of Mr Bottomley

TRANSPORT Questions are the end. They tend to bring out all those members who like discussing the quickest route from A to B or the disgraceful price of air travel or, worst of all, the pros and cons of the Channel tunnel. Every now and then they crack a joke to show that they too can see the funny side of things.

Sitting through Transport Questions is a bit like finding oneself stuck in a closed railway compartment with the entire team of BBC TV's *That's Life*. Does the minister have anything to say about road communications between Manchester and Sheffield? Does the minister understand that some road surfaces entail louder noise emissions? Does the minister understand the anger and frustration of many motorists?

After a few seconds of facing this sort of thing, any sane man would find tears of boredom trickling down his cheeks. Yet Mr Peter Bottomley, the present Minister for Roads, appears to relish every question, replying to them with undisguised glee.

With his little round glasses, schoolboy parting and cheeky smile, Mr Bottomley looks like a go-ahead vicar from a seaside postcard. Here, you would have thought, is a man who would happily lend you his bicycle clips, and might well inform an inquiring stranger of the prettiest route to the village green. It thus comes as quite a shock to hear him pontificate so enthusiastically on minimum tread depth for tyres or the new traffic consultants' report on the A59. These are subjects that should be kept from someone of such a transparently healthy frame of mind.

Mr Peter Bottomley was recently declared a "lunatic in swimming pants" by the distinguished editor of *The Literary Review*. Viewers peered avidly for signs of madness. At first, it seemed as if they might be disappointed: if he was wearing swimming pants at all, he had cunningly placed them underneath his conventional long trousers.

He smiles more often and less slyly than most of his colleagues, but that is to his credit. His tendency to bite his nails and to lace up his shoes while facing urgent cross-questioning is unusual, but less unusual than a tendency to lace up his nails or to bite his shoes. *21 June 1988*

Containing proposals for a new Party, and a Word or Two from Mr Hattersley

JUST as bakers must bake their daily buns, so MPs must moan their daily moan. In some respects, Members of Parliament represent a broad cross-section of the population. There are fat ones and thin ones, hairy ones and bald ones, Northerners and Southerners, drinkers and abstainers, and so on and so forth.

But here the similarity of MPs to normal human beings ends, for while the normal human does not care one way or the other about most political issues, the MP must have something to say about everything. The interests of the apathetic are wholly disregarded by the House of Commons. Rarely does an MP rise in the Chamber of the House to say, "To be honest, I'm not quite sure what I feel about that one". No, they are all little Jack-in-the-boxes, leaping up and down and around and around and from side to side and back to front, getting het up about whatever issue is available.

This leaves normal observers at a considerable disadvantage; the House has a setting, a history, good scenery, a wide variety of characters, even a plot of sorts, but it could never become a great success because it has no-one with whom the average viewer can relate. Everyone in the Chamber is either for or against whatever is presented to them. Like fussy eaters, they either have to spit out or eulogize over every dish that is served, while their fellow humans are quite happy to nibble away without a murmur.

Even the future of a pretty railway line becoms a political issue worth chomping away at, something you are either for or against. "Unimaginative and vicious" and "heavy-handed and uncaring", declared Mr Bob Cryer, of the privatization of the Settle-Carlisle railway.

The double-adjective outcry is a favourite of members, so that things are never just bad but "bad and uncaring", never just good but "good and caring". Oh, for the member for Apathy South to mumble offhandedly from a sedentary position that someting was "a bit caring and a bit uncaring" or "not so good, but then again not so bad". In its one-page manifesto (*Can't Complain: A Future in Apathy*), the Apathy Party, having pledged to leave well alone, might also agree not to waste too much time in their constituencies or in the Chamber, but to put their heads around the door at least once in a while.

But back to the Settle-Carlisle railway. Mr David Mitchell, Minister of State for Transport, having first pretended to be for it, turned out to be against it. Championing the new Conservative philosophy, which stridently argues against all conservation, Mr Mitchell declared that British Rail was interested in "investing in the twenty-first century and not in providing pleasure rides for railway archaeologists", spitting out the key three words – pleasure, railway, archaeologists – as if they were the very lowest of the low.

[71]

"Wholly unacceptable" and "wholly unshootable". Why, if it wasn't Mr Roy Hattersley back at the Despatch Box, lips once more aquiver at a pronouncement by Mr Hurd! After the Settle-Carlisle railway came Mr Hurd barking his announcement of a new organization, the Broadcasting Standards Council, to view all sex and violence before others have a chance. "Dangerous and absurd" was Mr Hattersley's double-adjective outcry, countered by Mr Hurd with a "grossly unjust".

"A combination of the patrician and the philistine", complained a Labour backbencher, and by this time everyone was hot under the collar over the idea that Sir William Rees-Mogg should be watching so much sex and violence, an activity for which the Labour benches believed him to be wholly unshootable.

Finally, Mr Hurd accused Mr Hattersley of "trying to stir up a storm in a tea cup". But which politician, handed a tea cup, does not puff and blow and tremble and shake, never fully satisfied until all the waves of tea have landed ker-plosh upon his neighbour's lap?   *17 May 1988*

×∞∞∞∞∞∞∞∞∞∞∞∞∞∞∞∞∞∞∞∞∞∞∞∞∞∞∞∞∞∞∞∞∞∞∞∞∞∞∞×

Transport Questions
Containing curious echoes of the previous Sketch, with some Fresh thoughts from Mr Bottomley

WHILST others are happy to hold faint grudges, MPs prefer to call for a change in the law. On a half-hour walk to work, the average MP will have spotted up to 10 aspects of modern life that cry out for instant legislation: the noise from a Sony Walkman, the litter in the gutter, the demands of a pamphleteer, a car parked on a kerb, an excess of skips, a building in the wrong place, the smell from a hamburger stall, a late bus, an early bus, a loose paving stone.

At a glance, few who use car telephones look wholly admirable characters; most people who have observed them in their self-important conversations will have felt a twinge of irritation from time to time. But only an MP could grow sufficiently incensed to attempt to ban the objects of their pleasure. Mr David Amess (Con, Basildon) wished to asked the Secretary of State for Transport "what representations he has received regarding the road safety implications of the use of car telephones".

Mr Peter Bottomley, the Under Secretary of State, revealed that he had received no representations. MPs tend to think that those who are not MPs spend their daily lives absolving this defect by making representations to MPs, and they seem constantly surprised to discover that this is not the case.

Mr Bottomley added that "if you can afford a car phone, you can afford a hands-free microphone". This was hardly a conclusion: if you can afford a car phone, you can afford 300 fluffy dice, 150 dogs with wobbly heads or 50 car horns that play the first few bars of "Colonel Bogey", but none of these will put a stop to the irritation to passers-by.

Mr Amess would not let the matter rest. He voiced concern following "drivers using phones while going down the motorway and turning corners". Turning corners on a motorway, even without making a telephone call, can be a chancy business and Mr Bottomley felt strongly enough to quote from the *Highway Code*. "Do not use a hand-held telephone when you are driving".

And there, you might have thought, the discussion would have ended. But this was the House of Commons, so of course it did not. Whenever a matter seems to be growing too frivolous, Mr Tony Banks (Lab, Newham North West) likes to add his own piece of folk wisdom, thus ensuring that it becomes utterly trivial. "Anyone who goes in a car holding a telephone and talking into it looks a right wally anyway", he chipped in.

Alas, the awful spirit of gravity, always hovering some way above Mr Banks, now dropped its grim tidings upon his head, causing him to ask Mr Bottomley for statistical evidence of accidents caused by car telephones.

The wacky world of Westminster is awash with statistics for this, that and the other. Immediately following this discussion, for instance, Mr Bottomley informed the House that the time taken for the average passenger to board the average London bus had been reduced from 4 seconds to 3.7 seconds. But Mr Bottomley regretfully announced that he had no statistics for accidents caused by car telephones.

He offered the House consolation, however, with "anecdotal evidence" concerning a taxi he had taken to Guildford. The taxi driver had been using a hand-held telephone and had shot through a red light. Literary experts in the House judged this as unlikely to make the pages of The Oxford Book of Car Telephone Anecdotes, but at least it made a break from statistics.

In an otherwise perfect three-minute microcosm of the parliamentary day – a mish-mash of furious demands for legislation, poor jokes, statistical evidence, personal anecdote, severe warnings of impending danger and sage ministerial advice – there was still something missing. Now what was it? Mr Jeremy Hanley (Con, Richmond and Barnes) rose to provide the absent ingredient.

If it was now acknowledged that car telephones could be dangerous, was it not time to take steps to stop people smoking in cars? The Parliamentary anti-smokers can be a terrible nuisance; no matter how well-aired the discussion, their arguments seem to cling to everything.   *15 March 1988*

Employment Questions
A brief Sketch containing Historical observation and a new Peer

AFTER the walk-outs and the shout-ins, the fall-outs and the lie-ins of the last week or two, dullness has returned at last to the Commons. This might well be connected with the afternoon's entry of Sir James Callaghan into the House of Lords, to emerge as Lord Callaghan of Cardiff. For his new Lordship, 1979 represented a peak in his country's fortunes, the general election of that year providing solid evidence that a sizeable minority of the electorate fully supported the direction and policies of the Labour Government.

Less loyal Labour supporters wonder whether it was quite such a great year after all. Sensing this, whenever the Opposition is looking pleased with itself, the Government lets loose the mischievous words "in 1979", and, like a mouse thrown into a vicarage tea party, it never fails to cause a stir.

Mr Norman Fowler is almost as keen on saying "in 1979" as he is on employing the phrase, "The fact of the matter is. . .". If he can begin a riposte, "The fact of the matter is, in 1979. . ." then he becomes doubly content.

The Tory version of history asserts that everything has got much, much better since 1979. When this version is challenged with statistics, Tory historians proclaim that everything that has got worse can be blamed fairly and squarely on the shoddy future planning of the last Labour government.

If little money was now being spent on training courses, the fact of the matter was that even less money was being spent in 1979. But weren't one million highly skilled, well-paid jobs now being replaced by non-skilled, lowly-paid jobs? "I don't accept that at all", spluttered Mr Fowler. "The fact of the matter is – ".

Labour murmurings were threatening to drown out whatever the fact of the matter might have been, so Mr Fowler repeated, pointing downwards with his forefinger: "The fact of the matter is that unemployment is going down."   *18 November 1987*

In which Mr Average confronts Mr Average and more fun is poked at Mr Maclennan

WHEN the House of Commons is televised, viewers may well be surprised at the number of repeats that appear on their screens. There are only around 12 different episodes ever recorded, and these are repeated, with occasional changes of character, throughout the parliamentary year.

The confrontation between Mr Meacher and Mr Fowler – Mr Average Meets Mr Average – is exactly the same every time it is shown.

The storyline is very simple. Mr Fowler boasts about a drop in unemployment. Mr Meacher claims that he's cooked the books. A Tory backbencher claims proudly that there are a number of people in employment in a constituency known to him. A Labour backbencher claims that everyone in the country is unemployed bar a select handful of Tory sympathizers. A Tory backbencher presents evidence to suggest that the vast majority of those claiming unemployment benefit own large country estates. And so it goes on.

Occasionally, a character who has been written out of a couple of episodes makes a dramatic return. Yesterday saw the return of Mr Dave Nellist, a man whose earnest, hairy presence suggests that he has made his home in some small, forgotten area of Hyde Park where Free Festivals celebrating the Spirit of '68 are still held on a daily basis. Indeed, it may well be that Mr Nellist is himself the Spirit of '68, for his ashen presence continues to haunt the Chamber, belting out forgotten numbers from the songbook of Blind Faith, such as "What About the Workers?" and "It's Disgusting".

Yesterday's episode saw Mr Nellist disgusted again. He said he'd like to see the day when every Tory MP had only one job and stopped lecturing the working classes on moonlighting. Seen it! Seen it! normal viewers might have cried, reaching for their control switches, but the members opposite seemed delighted by this chance to catch up on such a well-loved repeat, hooting with joy and laughter.

The next programme brought out a similar sense of *dèjà vu*. It was Prime Minister's Question Time, the quiz show with a difference – the difference being that there are never any answers.

Mr Harry Greenway (Con, Ealing North) crawled to his feet, rubbing his hands, his infamously long purple necktie struggling to spread across the floor in a budget reconstruction of Sir Walter Raleigh's gallant meeting with Good Queen Bess. "May I congratulate the Right Honourable Lady on entering her tenth year as Prime Minister and may I wish her many more," he grovelled uncontrollably. Alas, his moving love letter was disturbed by raucous hoots of "Sir Harry! Sir Harry!" from the unbelievers opposite.

The Speaker announced the next contestant. "Mr Robert MACLAREN" he boomed. Up stood Mr Robert Maclennan. Studio laughter rose and rose: 'Waahaahaa. WAAHAAHAA!" Mr Maclennan, the seasoned viewer may remember, last year experienced the sort of rise to fame normally confined to the storybooks. A minor member of the chorus, he stepped into the Leader's shoes just before the curtains went up and became, in true storybook fashion, a complete disaster. And now The Speaker himself had forgotten his name! Many are now arguing that the excessive humiliation of so upstanding a figure is fast becoming wholly unsuitable for the younger and more impressionable viewer.

Once Mr Maclennan had finished making the sort of mature, considered, sensitive point that is so hard to recall, even seconds after it has been uttered, a little Tory backbencher continued the series of repeats by praising the Prime Minister in exactly the same terms as had been used by another little Tory backbencher only a week before. Again they howled with laughter, leaving the absent minded, or perhaps simply absent, backbencher looking not a little bemused.

With Light Entertainment over for the day, the Heavy Entertainment lumbered to his feet. Mr Roy Hattersley, standing in for Mr Kinnock, opened his mouth to put a few well-rounded points to the Prime Minister. It was time to switch off. *4 May 1988*

<hr>

Arts Questions
Containing much Politeness

LITTLE white lies flit about the Chamber at all times of the day and night, but they are never so frisky as when Mr Richard Luce is in attendance. Mr Luce holds two important jobs. He is both Minister for the Arts and Minister for the Civil Service. Once a fortnight, Questions to the former are followed by Questions to the latter, each lasting just ten minutes.

Both sets of Questions appeal to the nosey parkers of the House. Arty questioners are forever asking poor Mr Luce whether he will be visiting exciting new theatre workshops in their constituencies. If he has already visited them, they ask him the even more difficult question of whether he enjoyed it. Cue fib. Civil Service questioners tend to see corruption and conspiracy behind every contract awarded and, if no contract has been awarded in the last few minutes, they fall back on Westland. By the end of each 20-minute section, Mr Luce has all of his fingers crossed, and the vast majority of his toes.

But Mr Luce seems the easy-going type and is adept at the art of the social compliment. "Darling, you simply must tell me the name of your hairdresser", he would say to Medusa as she swanned into the room. If this is a lie, it is only a very little one and as white as can be, for it reassures Medusa that somebody, somewhere is capable of appreciating her finer points.

When the subject of artistic exchange deals with the Soviet Union came up, Mr Roland Boyes asked whether, in the light of the recent "brilliant" exhibition of members' photographs, the Minister would try to organise an exchange exhibition with snap-happy Russian politicians. Like many amateur photographers, Mr Boyes can never stop going on about it. Sadly, the standard of members' efforts falls far short of his claims; the recent exhibition was full of wonky photos of the Taj Mahal, murky silhouettes of seagulls, gaudy sunsets, and so on. But that nice Mr Luce would never say as much. Instead he kept a straight face and cooed about how much he admired "the artistic quality and ability of members in this chamber".

Mr Luce's admiration for everyone and everything is quite boundless. A few minutes later, Mr Teddy Taylor popped up from his seat, demanding that he extend it to the Civil Servants of Southend. One of the most intriguing political enigmas of the post-war years is how Mr Taylor came by his Christian name, for it would be hard to imagine anyone less like a Teddy. A child pressing his tummy in the hope of a jolly squeak would be more likely to be greeted with a sharp clip around the ear. So it was understandable that Mr Luce should attempt to keep Teddy at arms length, resisting all temptations for a quick cuddle. Yes, "I enjoyed my visit to Southend and admired the work being done by the Civil Servants there", he said.   *5 July 1988*

In which Boredom may be Detected

SOME days are awfully dull. Only a smattering of members bother to turn up, and, of these, only one or two are recognizable. Observers look around for seasoned political experts to help them with the names of the others, only to find that they have stealthily slipped away: why else become a seasoned political expert, if not to possess the knowledge to vanish when boredom beckons?

These are the days when the all-seasons comedy turns – Skinner, Banks, Soames – decide that they are destined not for a cameo in a Carry On, but for a major Shakespearean role. Their questions substitute stodge for zip, the earnest for the jocular. They end up as Shakespearean as Barbara Windsor quoting Hamlet.

Elsewhere, quite sensible questions give rise to quite sensible answers, both questions and answers full to the brim with accurate percentage rises, statistical predictions and interim reports.

It was one of those days. Mr Eric Heffer lumbered to his feet with a complaint. "It's about time. . ." he began. This is the way he always begins.

"It's about time the people of this country realized. . ." he continued. This is the way he always continues. "It's about time the people of this country realized that this Government is only interested in profit", he ended. This is the way he always ends.

Mr Richard Holt (Con, Langbaurgh) asked "What is the Government's thinking in connection with windows?" Perhaps it was misheard. One can see that widows might come into the Government's thoughts, and even winos could be worth a bit of legislation, but it was hard to see how windows could be either a good thing or a bad thing.

Was this a planted question, designed to smooth the path for a ministerial announcement on the abolition of windows, thus giving a much-needed boost to the wall-paint industry? No – it emerged that Mr Holt was worried about heat loss. Not terribly worried. Just a bit.

Even though they last only ten minutes, Questions to the Minister of Arts usually provide drama, light entertainment, laughter, tears and time for a couple of quick choruses; but not today. Mrs Ewing (Scottish Nationalist, Moray) asked him not to overlook the minority cultures "such as Gallic". Again, Gillick or even garlic might have afforded some controversy, but never Gallic. The minister smiled genially. He wouldn't.

Mr Tony Banks, usually a good joker, uplifted his bonnet to let a tired old bee bumble its way to the floor. The Parthenon Marbles, as he calls them, should be returned "to eliminate a legacy of bitterness". Not many jokes there, you will agree. "If you start down that road, the question is – where do you end?" said the minister.

Mr Norman Fowler rose to answer Mr Michael Meacher's questions about a miscalculation of one tenth of one per cent in the monthly Retail Price Index. It began to look like the winning entry for a *Spectator* Weekend Competition for the most boring exchange in parliamentary history. This was followed by nearly an hour of Mr Bob Clay (Lab, Sunderland N) calling attention to unemployment.

Outside the Chamber, a Labour Party Press Release announced that a Mr David Clarke MP would be speaking at the launch of The Ramblers Association leaflet *Hedgerows – Lifelines of Our Countryside*. At last, a ray of sunshine.   *15 December 1987*

In which Miss Diane Arbus makes an Unexpected Appearance

NINE female artists have been exhibited at the Tate Gallery since 1910, compared with 200 male artists, stormed Mrs Ann Clwyd (Lab, Cynon Valley). This sort of statistic, coming from female colleagues, fusses the men on the Labour benches. They are duty bound to come up with something even more devastating in its unfairness to women, both as a proof of their solidarity and as a confession of their collective male guilt.

Mr Mark Fisher, Opposition spokesman on the arts, had an awful statistic to announce to the House. The Hayward Gallery had never given an exhibition to a woman at all.

Those in the Press Gallery, professionally attracted to scenes of devastation, horror and mental imbalance, recalled with indignation the 1975 exhibition of Ms Diane Arbus's photographs at the Hayward Gallery. Men with spotty faces and manic grins, women with unkempt hair and desperate eyes, married couples in horrible discord: all were pictured in unforgiving black-and-white. If Ms Arbus were still alive, many felt, she would be just the person to instigate illustrative snapshots in the somewhat wordy pages of Hansard.

Making amends for their ignorance of a woman so close to their souls, members on all sides became unconscious Living Exhibits in an impromptu Diane Arbus Retrospective. First in the catalogue was "Could I Just Make One Other Point?", an unnerving scenario featuring Mr Cecil Parkinson as newly-appointed Secretary of State for Energy.

The overall effect of disquiet emerging from the figure is heightened by the disparity of the smooth exterior and the inner turmoil. A spritely new double-breasted suit, a spotty silk tie immaculately knotted, a perfectly judged parting in the hair – all these are tragically undermined by the large, nervous hands pulling at the socks, the endlessly nodding and bobbing head, the twitchy, mask-like smile, the restless eyes. This is indeed a disturbing study of the anxiety beneath the surface of life in the twentieth century, and deserves comparison with the earlier works of Goya and Velázquez.

"I Would Like to Visit Leicester Again Before Too Long" is the darkly ironic introductory title given to the Second Exhibit, Mr Richard Luce, Minister for the Arts. Why would he like to visit Leicester again before too long? This is a question that – in the manner of Pinter or Beckett – is never answered wholly satisfactorily but remains an enigma to the end. His ostensible reason, that the reputation of Leicester Haymarket Theatre provides sufficient temptation for a return, is surely intended to tantalize by its very unlikelihood. Skilful play is made on other themes: feminism, sponsorship, standards of excellence; but the overall picture is one of irreconcilable differences between dreams and reality.

A number of derivative and unremarkable miniatures, "Full Consultation with All Involved", "Frustration of the Ordinary Man and Woman in the Street", "The Important Contribution of the Civil Service", can be skipped over, but then we arrive at "One Rule for the Rich and Another for the Poor", an illuminating study of Mr Dennis Skinner in the manner of Mr Diego Rivera, with a mass of contemporary allusions to the sins of the rich: Mr Keith Best and his Shares, Captain Mark Phillips and his Car, the Massed Army of City Whizz-Kids, surrounding the loud central icon, representing in its unashamed brashness The True Voice of the People.

The exhibition closes on a sombre, almost apocalyptic note with a full-length version of Mr John Moore, the only Tory whose elocution has reached such a high pitch that when he pronounces the word "guarantee" one can clearly hear the sound of the letter "u". As he talks on and on, the spectator finds himself falling asleep. Aha! But this is surely the very purpose of this bleak and desolate exhibition.   *3 November 1987*

><><><><><><><><><><><><><><><><><><><><><><><><><><><><><><><><><><><><><><><><

Foreign Office Questions
In which the childish sport of Batty Book Titles is pursued

THE *New Statesman* recently staged a weekend competition for unlikely book titles. One of the winners was *Playboy Diplomat: The Life of Sir Geoffrey Howe*. This seems a mite harsh. While Sir Geoffrey is rarely seen diving into New York night-clubs on the arms of Princess Stephanie of Monaco, he has a pleasant, bumbling manner which might well find him hobnobbing on occasion with some of the more risqué European Agricultural Ministers.

But some think that his liaisons with dusky Europeans have already gone far enough. Mr Ian Gow (*A Wild and Crazy Guy: The Middle Years of Ian Gow*) was up to no good. "There are many of us who view with dismay the replacement of the British passport with the common EEC passport", he boomed, adding, "The day of the nation state is not yet over!"

Sir Geoffrey looked a little surprised. If his wrist-watch was correct, his expression seemed to imply, the day of the nation state had only a few more minutes to go. But he tends to avoid the cut-and-thrust of politics, preferring the mutter-and-snooze approach, so he made every effort to bore his way out of Mr Gow's quaint old English cul-de-sac.

"There is a wide range of feeling about the pattern which might be followed in the. . .", he began, and already the most highly motivated of whirling dervishes would have found himself dreaming of Horlicks and a spot of shut-eye. ". . .development of the EEC", he continued. "The original agreement that there should be a common-format passport was made as long ago as 1975 by the then Prime Minister."

"The then Prime Minister"? To whom could he be referring? Even the most experienced of political observers find their memories clogging up when forced to recall the appointments of such an age gone by. Wasn't Mr Eric Morecambe Prime Minister for a short time in the mid-Seventies? Or perhaps Miss Noele Gordon? It took the razor-sharp historical prowess of Mr Jonathan Aitken (*My Mission to Explain: The Autobiography of Jonathan Aitken*) to come up with the correct answer.

"It's been a long time since we've had a British Tory Foreign Secretary sheltering behind the coat-tails of Sir Harold Wilson!" he exclaimed. Ah yes! Harold Wilson (*The Governance of Britain*)! Funny little fellow. Smoked a pipe. Long forgotten. Once met Cilla Black. Alas, Sir Geoffrey grew huffy at the analogy. "There's no question of my sheltering behind anyone's coat-tails, least of all Sir Harold Wilson's", he began.

In his next few breaths, the full measure of Sir Geoffrey's annoyance could be gauged. Having said, "least of all *Sir* Harold Wilson's", he corrected himself. "Lord Wilson", he said. And then: "So sorry – Lord Wilson of Rievaulx." (This he pronounced with a contempt more usually reserved for used tissues found buried in forgotten pockets). And finally: "The Right Honourable and Noble Lord Wilson of Rievaulx". It is indicative of the usefulness of Sir Geoffrey's reticence that simply by groping his way through the rich and varied absurdities of someone's title he can reduce a reputation to nothing.

Foreign Office Questions plodded on. Sir Bernard Braine (*A Giggle or Two with Sir Bernie: Light-hearted Recollections of a Life in Politics*) thundered about the fate of the former Imperial Family of Ethiopia, his fulminations prompting his colleague Mr Neil Hamilton (*The Quest for Truth: An Appreciation of the BBC in the Eighties*) to a speedy impersonation.

The mere mention of the Sharpeville Six guarantees the sight of Tory Ogres leaping up and down in their seats, baring their teeth in pantomime style. Mr John Carlisle (*Biko My Brother*) vied for attention with Mr Eric Forth (*My Life in Reggae*), but the Speaker called Mr Forth.

Mr Forth wished to know whether Mrs Chalker had congratulated the South African Government on the independence of its judiciary. For Mr Forth, this was mild indeed. In no time at all, he will be co-authoring *Bonnie Tidings from The Land of Porridge: The Labour Left in Scotland* with Mr Ron Brown.   *5 May 1988*

Welsh Questions
Containing a brief glimpse into the Life and Times of Mr Eric Heffer

LIKE Mr Clark Kent or, to some extent, Ms Lois Lane, there's not a lot that Mr Eric Heffer hasn't done. With each fresh question he asks, he reveals yet another stitch in the long and varied tapestry of his life.

"As somebody who. . ." his questions invariably begin, and eager observers lean forward to tune in to the latest episode from the Life and Times of Eric Heffer. These opportunities are not to be sniffed at, for, if Mr Benn's leadership bid is successful, then we may yet see Mr Heffer occupying Mr Lawson's trousers.

"As somebody who. . ." There follows any section or sections from a curriculum vitae of quite outstanding merit and distinction. On one day Mr Heffer might present himself as somebody who has spent all his adult life combatting injustice and oppression; on another he will stand as somebody who has travelled as far as Scotland or the Continent; and on yet another he will speak as somebody who has been a lifelong employer of the ballpoint pen.

Inevitably, some of these proud boasts are rather more interesting than others. "As somebody who. . ." he began a question yesterday, and his aspirant biographers began to take notes. "As somebody who actually studied the Welsh language on a Liverpool University extra mural course. . ." he continued. In Heffer terms, this is hot stuff, and it was to grow even hotter. ". . .and as somebody who is a member of the Welsh Labour History Society. . ." Gasp! Almost as he spoke, publishers were frantically ordering reams upon reams of extra paper, so as to be in a position to rush out more copies of "Heffer: The Welsh Language Years, Volume One" in time for Christmas.

Mr Heffer asked the Secretary of State for Wales what efforts were being made to encourage the study of his beloved Welsh language in areas outside Wales, "in particular in England". From then on, Hefferless, Welsh Questions were back on tear-jerkingly tedious form, the mad bark of Mr Peter Walker doing little to ruffle the gabble-gabble-gabble of the Welsh hens.

As usual during Welsh Questions, those Tory MPs who had wandered into the Chamber, presumably by mistake, found that their eyelids soon began to droop. Yet Mr Harry Greenway's eyes were as beady as ever, his schoolmasterly hand wrapped around a fountain pen, busying away with making notes. An unlikely Boswell to Heffer's Johnson, Mr Greenway (Con, Ealing North) seemed more probably engaged in preparing his own question to The Member Representing the Church Commissioners, Mr Michael Alison.

With only five minutes in every fortnight to rule the roost, The Member Representing the Church Commissioners occupies a similar position in The House of Commons as "The Sky at Night" occupies on BBC Television. It must be particularly galling for poor Mr Alison that so much of his precious space seems always to be occupied by the Milky Ways of Mr Greenway.

Mr Greenway is worried by most things that happen in Church, and by much that happens out of it. A vicar cannot express himself as pleased to see the sun shining so brightly without Mr Greenway bouncing up to condemn the modern trend among clergymen to interfere in matters over which they have no jurisdiction. Yesterday Mr Greenway declared himself upset that the efforts from the Church in the countryside were funding the leftward-inclined "Faith in the Cities" schemes. There, there, went Mr Alison.

One of the many earthly glories of questions to Mr Alison is that they signal the end of Welsh Questions for another two weeks. Alas, once Welsh members have begun to talk of their favourite subject they find it hard to stop. With Mr Alison's five minutes over, Mrs Ann Clwyd (Lab, Cynon Valley) rose to ask Mr John Wakeham why there was no Welsh bottled water in the House. "As somebody who likes to drink Welsh water whenever I can. . ." began Mr Wakeham, and Mr Heffer could be seen to lean forward, perhaps envious of such biographical distinction in a member of the Tory Cabinet.   *26 April 1988*

<hr>

Northern Ireland Questions
In which Mr Paisley is compared both to a Bisto Kid and Uncle Mac, though with little accuracy

ONE OF the many oddities about Mr Paisley is the amount of smiling he gets up to. He smiles so much, and so energetically, that in a better world he might have been usefully employed in advertisements for leading brands of toothpaste, or perhaps as a Northern Irish Bisto Kid. Another oddity concerns the speed with which his smile can turn into a scowl, and then back to a smile once more, without any of the conventional facial contortions or hesitations in between.

His visits to the Chamber of the House of Commons are rare, but he puts them to good use. He sits on the Tory benches beside the eerie figure of Mr Peter Robinson. While Mr Robinson sits upright, thin and expressionless, Mr Paisley spends much of his time lolloping on his corner seat, his legs outstretched, a chuckle playing on his lips, perusing his order paper. Sometimes he looks for all the world like Uncle Mac rejoicing in fond

memories of the last Teddy Bears' Picnic. But kiddies on all sides of the House would be well advised not to offer this particular Uncle Mac a cookie. His large and sudden bites can often incorporate a hand or two. Then, munching on the hand, he will issue one of his red-faced and scornful chuckles, and the whole House will shudder to its very bones.

Questions to the Secretary of State for Northern Ireland are a particular favourite of Mr Paisley. Over the years, he has shown a lively personal interest in the affairs of Northern Ireland, and he likes to seek a cheery word of advice from that nice Mr King whenever he can. Before he asks a question, he wipes the chuckle off his face, swallows any hands he might be chewing, leans forward in his seat and does his best to look fearsome. His best happens to be very good indeed. He then looms to his feet, his vast bulk casting a shadow over the Chamber, and that nice Mr King begins to look a little worried.

Yesterday Mr Paisley wished to know whether Mr King agreed with the Prime Minister, who believed Mr Haughey had been out of order in his recent speech, or the Foreign Secretary, who believed he had spoken as a patriot. Mr Paisley's questions are notable, among other things, for their volume. They are delivered at a pitch more normally reserved for the issuing of warnings at sea, or the take-off of a lunar rocket.

That nice Mr King replied that he agreed with them both, and that he saw no contradiction between the two points of view.

"Of course you wouldn't!" boomed Mr Paisley from his corner, his face reddening, his scowl growing ever more carnivorous. But within a few seconds he was back to his old smiling self, exchanging giggles with Mr Robinson – a process similar, one might have thought, to exchanging giggles with one of the less outgoing inhabitants of the Chamber of Horrors.

When Mr Kevin McNamara, Shadow Minister for Northern Ireland, bumbled to his feet, Mr Paisley looked as cheery as if Mr Pastry had appeared, which, in a way, he had. Mr McNamara is a white-haired figure of increasing comic potential, always opening barn doors so that horses may bolt, forever cooking up objections way after each issue has passed. Having failed to bat an eyelid at the original announcement of the Gibraltar killings, he has recently taken to batting both eyelids with such vehemence that many wish to call for a doctor. Make way! Make way! A doctor is at hand! Alas, it is only Doctor Paisley, laughing his guts out at Mr McNamara's every protestation.

A minute or two later, the Doubled-Up Doctor chose to megaphone his way through the ins and outs of a recent murder, 'a well organized inside job". Again, the red-faced scowl, and again, seconds later, the vulpine cackling. Beside him, Mr Robinson took to his feet. During Northern Ireland Questions, there always seems to be one of them up and one down. The two of them resemble nothing so much as a grotesque Swiss weather predictor, forever presaging gloom ahead. *29 April 1988*

Environment Questions
Containing a brief introduction to the bizarre Environment team

MRS Marion Roe, Mr Nicholas Ridley and Mr Colin Moynihan sit together on the front bench during Environment Questions, calling to mind a bizarre family of the type favoured by comedy producers.

First comes Mr Ridley, lanky, lip-curling, fed up to the back teeth with all those silly little questions. Then there is Mrs Roe, with the dress sense of Miss Esther Rantzen and the hair of Struwelpeter; her whole suggesting a sorty of groggy Mrs Thatcher, putting in an appearance in the House straight from a hard night out on the town. And between them, their bright little boy, young Colin Moynihan, doing so well for himself, and not yet out of shorts.

Usually it is Poll Tax this and Poll Tax that, and Mr Ridley sneers back his replies. But Poll Tax, like the Health Crisis and Unemployment, now seems largely forgotten by the Opposition, and poor Mr Ridley has been running around, like a dog looking for a postman, in search of other complaints to savage. "I'm surprised the Honourable Lady asks such a stupid question," he snapped at someone who asked him whether he would like to live in a cardboard box under Waterloo Bridge. By next week he will have dreamed up a new Cardboard Box (Mobile Housing Tax) Bill so that he once again basks in the fear and loathing of the Opposition.

A minute or two later, a Labour member said that it was about time Mr Moynihan "spoke up for our national game of football". The time was ripe for Mr Moynihan to deliver his Churchillian oration. "I will always speak up for successes," he vowed, "and I will always speak out against hooliganism!" There were probably millions of people outside the House who shared his view, but the handful of people inside the House found it curiously lacking in zip. Only when Mr Moynihan speaks out against successes and speaks up for hooliganism will he have earned himself sufficient all-party venom to be seen as a worthy successor to his mentor, Mr Ridley. *19 May 1988*

In which Mr Geoffrey Dickens predicts a Plague of Locusts

QUESTION: What does a scourge do? Answer: It sweeps the country. In the catechism of the backbench Tory, a fresh scourge of one thing or another sweeps the country every couple of days.

Mr Geoffrey Dickens is the most noted scourgepiracy theorist. Every morning, as he tumbles out of bed and draws back the curtains, something new and awful catches his eye. Down in the Dickens garden, the beasties are ever at play. Recently, he has sighted witches, and before them child molesters, and, only a day or two ago, plagues of locusts. They are all, of course, dead on course to "sweep the country".

Though Mr Dickens, vast, common and creepy, is the most obviously grotesque of the scourgepiracy theorists, he is not alone. Rather, he is the carved ghoul on a packed trunk of populist Conservative fearaticians. Somewhere in this grisly caseload lies Mr Tony Favell (Con, Stockport) who, perhaps unduly affected by standing in the 1979 General Election against The Beast of Bolsover, tends to see a scourge behind every hedge.

During Environment Questions, Mr Favell announced that graffiti was a "scourge sweeping the country". Since Tories never feel that anything really exists until it can be proved to cost millions of pounds, he began to count the cost. The graffiti scourge had cost "Birmingham Buses alone" two million pounds, and was costing the rest of the country a clear one and a half thousand million pounds. Quite how he had totted it all up he did not let on, but his figures went down a bomb with fellow backbenchers. It was time for the law to "take its gloves off", boomed Mr Favell. This type of speech always ends with a call to ban something or other. Sure enough, Mr Favell called for a ban on the sale of all aerosols to the under-16s.

In this comprehensive and diligently researched roundup of the Parliamentary fearaticians, it would be unfair not to mention Mr Joe Ashton. Mr Ashton is a Labour member of the straight-talking, never-did-me-any-harm, voice-of-common-sense school of politicians, a sort of Geoffrey Dickens who found himself placed on the left rather than the right when the gnarled and jittery hand of politics was dealing its tuppenny-ha'penny deck. He likes to think that he talks nitty-gritty, though skilled observers detect in his speeches rather more of the nitty than of the gritty.

As might have been expected, Mr Ashton had a thing or two to say on the subject of graffiti. He claimed that just as laws to make citizens sign for garden poisons had "cut down on murderers", so a law to make them sign for spray paint would cut down on graffiti. Under an Ashton regime it is quite possible that everything would be signed for: rope, to cut down on strangling, telephones, to cut down on obscene calls, water, to cut down on murder-by-drowning, and so on. But Mr Nicholas Winterton did not think that Mr Ashton went nearly far enough.

Whenever Mr Winterton sees a bend, he goes round it. Though he may not yet be quite mad, he is certainly already barking. "Ruff! Ruff! Ruff!" goes his voice, while his face grows steadily redder and redder. Nothing for Mr Winterton is ever quite acceptable. Indeed, everything is "quite unacceptable". It was, he thought, "quite unacceptable that retail outlets accept no responsibility for what they sell". Warming to his subject, he demanded "a bit of hard labour" for offenders, and, his bark growing louder and louder, he wanted to see these youths forced to "remove what they have done to DESECRATE THE COMMUNITY!!!"

Mr Merlyn Rees seemed an unlikely fellow to be caught mixing with this rabble of spray-speakers. It was rather as if King Lear had been snapped whooping it up with a bevy of drunken can-can girls. Mr Rees said that he wished to point out that the underpasses of Elephant and Castle were "indescribable" as they were "smothered in graffiti". With such distress being caused even to the sane by this terrible muck, it is most surely time for all Mr Geoffrey Dickens's witches to pick up their brooms and join forces to sweep the country. *23 June 1988*

In which the Sketchwriter notices Fascinating similarities between Two Politicians divided only by the Atlantic Ocean

DISTRACTED, perhaps, by the comings and goings of the Leader of the Opposition over the last few weeks, seasoned political commentators have devoted curiously little space to a full examination of the uncanny similarities between two distinguished politicians, one on this side of the Atlantic, the other in the United States. Though they come from different edges of the political spectrum, though one is white and the other black, their rhetorical skills have much in common. The two politicians are, of course, Mr Jesse Jackson, from the US, and Mr Nicholas Ridley, from Great Britain. It has now been possible to compare and contrast the styles of the two with some accuracy, as both have made important statements within the last 48 hours.

To some extent, it could be argued that Mr Jackson is the more outgoing of the two. Contrast, for instance, Mr Jackson's message to the Democratic Convention in Atlanta on Tuesday night ("I love you all, I love you all") with Mr Ridley's somewhat less effusive message to the House of Commons early yesterday afternoon ("If the Honourable Member were to look in Hansard he would see what a stupid question he has just asked").

The contrasting emotional reticence of Mr Ridley is further evidenced in his disinclination to draw on family ties. In his Atlanta oration, Mr Jackson referred to his family's arrival in America on a slave ship. Yesterday, Mr Ridley was encouraged by a Labour backbencher to make similar play with his own roots. When he visited Newcastle the next day, asked the backbencher, would he call at Ridley Place, named after his ancestors, and explain why (to paraphase) the rich had all the money?

Interestingly, Mr Ridley eschewed the appeal to the emotions upon which he has based so much of his career. Perhaps, in the past, the Ridley family had also made that trip to America on board a slave ship, albeit in the best deluxe cabin the cap'n could provide, but, if so, Mr Ridley decided against such pulling on the heartstrings. No: "What a stupid question," he said, preferring to leave it at that.

It is in their command of the physical gesture that Jackson and Ridley seem at times to be virtually the same man. As Mr Jackson says: "Keep hope alive! Keep hope alive! Keep hope alive!" tears well up in his eyes, his arms thrust forward and he looks to some far horizon. The same is true of Mr Ridley. As Mr Ridley says "What a stupid question" his tongue seems to well up in his mouth, it then darts forward through his lips and he pushes his glasses further onto his nose.

Just as the ghost of Dr Martin Luther King hovers behind Mr Jackson, so the ghost of Mr Nicholas Luther Soames can be seen chewing sweeties behind Mr Ridley. Both urge their earthly manifestations on to greater things: in Mr Jackson's case, greater hope for his people; in Mr Ridley's case, greater development of luxury maisonettes in the Green Belt. "We can call upon our noble instincts and navigate this vessel to safety" might have been Soames hobnobbing with Ridley, for both come from generations of Old Etonians and their mutual claims to nobility are unmatched. But, no! It is Jackson speaking to Dukakis! The very fact that such a muddle could occur demonstrates further the peculiar affinity between the two camps.

Mr Ridley is as adept as Mr Jackson when introducing a little American-style razzamatazz into his public appearances, occasionally even going so far as to smile, though only at the misfortunes of others. He is, above all, a salesman, silencing his natural foes with a powerful charm. When his opposite number, Dr Jack Cunningham, spoke against "record homeless-ness, spiralling house prices, and the return of Rachmanism" – implied criticism, according to experts – Mr Ridley had an answer. Following Mr Jackson's statement of dreams ("My work to keep American strong and make America better is ancient and endless"), Mr Ridley revealed his own hopes for the future. "We are pursuing a very tight land-use planning policy," he said, tears welling in his eyes.   *21 July 1988*

7

THE HOUSE OF LORDS

A brief Interlude in which the Sketchwriter puts his Head around the door of the Upper House, therein to witness all Manner of dignitaries, an excess of Politeness and the Compere of a television Quiz game

In which the sister of Her Majesty smiles graciously upon Norman, Baron St John of Fawsley of Preston Capes in our county of Northampton

RH Princess Margaret beamed graciously down from the Gallery as Mr Norman St John Stevas breathed his last. Dressed in his scarlet and ermine, he was about to become The Lord St John of Fawsley. He paraded slowly into the chamber of the House of Lords, the tips of his mouth veering downwards to the floor in the appropriate expression of gravitas.

Anyone less versed than Mr St John Stevas in the customs of the Palace of Westminster might have mistaken the ceremony for an impending judgement of execution. In front of him sat the new Lord Chancellor, a black tricorn hat perched atop his wig. To his left sat two Bishops, their hands clasped as if in prayer. Above him, a quantity of elegantly coiffed women looked down, their knitting happily absent.

"Norman Anthony Francis St John Stevas. . ." the name was pronounced with the solemnity of a call to the scaffold. But then came the good news. He was now Norman, Baron St John of Fawsley of Preston Capes in our county of Northampton.

After he had been sworn in, he followed his two sponsors, Lord Home of the Hirsel and Lord Charteris of Amisfield, to a side bench. There the three were conducted by a Jack of Diamonds in the repeated doffing of their hats in the direction of the Lord Chancellor. One doff, two doffs, three doffs: less sober figures performing the same actions in more vulgar surroundings would have come perilously close to resembling excitable holidaymakers yelling "That's All Folks!" in an Amateur Hour routine. But dignity was never safer than in these hands.

After the short ceremony was over, Lord St John of Fawsley disrobed and took his place among the sea of slightly familiar faces. Hugh Scanlon, Len Murray, Woodrow Wyatt, Keith Joseph: memory lane was never better populated. One half expected Mr Tommy Steele, Mr Reginald Kray, The Andrews Sisters and Mr Bobby Moore to be somewhere about the place.

How very much more comfortable the new Baron will be in his new environment! While members of the House of Commons were being chastised for their unseemly language, Their Lordships were exchanging compliments with one another on the excellence of the new report into their procedures. Introducing the report, Lord Whitelaw thanked the committee for their excellent work. Lord Aberdare thanked all the clerks and all their

[93]

Lordships who had taken the trouble to fill in the questionnaire. Everyone had been an immense help.

The gentlest massage on the temples at the end of a tiring day would seem as nothing beside the even tones of Lord Aberdare. Rarely has inoffensiveness given less offence. ". . .Some of your Lordships felt that Question Time was becoming somewhat rowdy; others found it interesting and lively. . .The difficulty is that whatever one peer believes to be important may not appear so to another. . ." Such calm and tranquillity in Another Place would be interrupted within seconds by the cackle of a Skinner or the phantom howl of a Dickens. "No doubt most of your Lordships prefer short speeches. . ." continued Lord Aberdare.

"Hear! Hear!" agreed their Lordships.

". . .particularly from others" added Lord Aberdare. By and large, the committee had decided that there was no need for too much change. If anyone spoke for more than the alloted fifteen minutes "discreet murmurings" might be more appropriate than any more draconian enforcement.

Lord Shackleton then praised the report as "very well written". He compared the good manners of the Lords with the unruly behaviour of the Commons. The only slightly harsh words he had for the Upper House were reserved for the lifts, which took two minutes to go up eleven floors. It would be awfully nice if they could go a bit faster. A gentle smile playing on his lips, Lord St John of Fawsley sat back in his seat, a man content.

5 November 1987

><><><><><><><><><><><><><><><><><><><><><><><><><><><><><><><><><><><><><><

Containing a Name-Dropper, a French President, and a pair of Fashionable Spectacles

IN HIS slip-on shoes, Lord Callaghan of Cardiff sat comfortably in his new home awaiting his turn to speak in a "Debate on the Progress Made in Disarmament Negotiations and the Improvement in East-West Relations".

"Hello. . .hello", he mouthed as past colleagues brushed past him to take their seats, his sunny smile now unclouded by the contradictions of office. Cross-legged, cross-armed, he listened appreciatively as Lord Cledwyn of Penhros, opening the debate, declared from the Labour benches: "We much look forward to the maiden speech of Lord Callaghan. . .how glad we are to see him in our House".

As Lord Cledwyn spoke of optimism, Lord Callaghan's eyes seemed fixed on a spot way above the Government benches, where the statue of a knight in armour resides, an angel fluttering at his feet. The knight has his right hand crossed over onto his left shoulder, in a manner reminiscent of

Lord Callaghan himself, though there the similarity stops: the knight wears no fashionably square-rimmed spectacles.

Unlike the House of Commons, where even a speech in favour of smiling would find at least on faction of diehard scowlers ready to shout it down, the House of Lords is at times as horribly polite as the most nightmarishly well-mannered little girl dreamed of by Saki.

We must all be grateful to the Noble Lord not only for this, but also for that, declared Lord Glenarthur, and such politeness became additionally terrifying when one realized he was speaking from the opposite bench. Observers more used to the Commons could not help but shudder in their seats.

"We shall certainly not solve overnight problems that have been with us for decades", announced the young Lord Glenarthur. Yes, yes, one wants to blurt out during many speeches in the Lords – but get to the point. The short, sharp, shocks of speeches that inhabit the Commons are replaced by long, burbling suffocations in the Lords. But Lord Callaghan seemed content to have the soft pillow of grandiloquent circumlocution placed snugly over his face. He shuffled his finger half-way up his cheek as if posing for a stately photograph, with his other hand withdrawing a packet of mints. He then popped one into his mouth. Within seconds he emerged as a chewer, not a sucker.

Lord Mayhew was now speaking; Lord Callaghan would be next. "Despite limited improvements the European members of Nato are still failing to get their act together", said Lord Mayhew, and Lord Callaghan began to twiddle his thumbs, Farmer Jim surveying his new acres. Suddenly Lord Len of Murray, Trades Unionist extraordinaire, put his head round the door, and, just as suddenly, put it back again.

"May I thank my noble Lords for the kindness and courtesy that has been shown to me. I ask that it be extended to me again for a short time this afternoon", said Lord Callaghan, his lips relishing this new opportunity to emit such traditional words of harmonious hob-nobbery with the highest.

"This is a moment to stand back", he said. Heedless of such advice, the Noble Lords around him preferred to sit and even lie back, their eyes half open. Following the indications in his recent autobiography that he is not only an ex-Prime Minister but also something of a glorified autograph-hunter, Lord Callaghan managed to smatter his speech with phrases such as, "As President Mitterrand repeated to me just two days ago. . .", juxtaposed with the avuncular ominiscience of "I trust the Prime Minister will banish any lingering doubts from her mind that. . ."

As he speaks his voice rises at the end of each sentence, giving the impression of one still surprised, and a little bit disappointed, that the rest of the world has not always seen fit to follow his lead.

". . .and greater understanding." So ended his speech. The Bishop of Rochester immediately commended it as "a speech to which many have been looking forward since the Noble Lord entered the House". This was a most Christian response. Some might even have thought a little too Christian, perhaps.   *10 December 1987*

Lord Young's cuffs appear to Twinkle in the sunlight while Lord Longford comforts an Offender

IN MANY respects, Lord Young of Graffham bears an uncanny resemblance to Mr Michael Miles, the influential television quizmaster who became widely known in the mid-to-late 1960s for his popular programme, "Take Your Pick". Within this extraordinary similarity – up until now largely ignored by political commentators – there might well lie a clue to the character of the present Secretary of State for Trade and Industry. Yes or no?

Yes. Gong! It was, of course, one of Mr Miles's guiding rules that his contestants should never utter the words "yes" or "no". If ever they did, the gong would bang, and off they would be led. Lord Young sticks rigidly by Mr Miles's principles, applying them to himself with an even greater rigour than he demands of others.

Yesterday, the quizmaster was to become the quizzed when he was due to be called to account for himself in a Private Notice Question from Lord Shackleton. Lord Shackleton believes that Lord Young deceived the House when he implied that there was no deadline to British involvement in the Canadian Radarsat satellite project. Lord Young says he did not. Yes or no?

A few minutes before he was due on, Lord Young trotted into the Chamber of the House of Lords with a brisk and confident air, nodding this way and that to the ranks of panellists, his traditional red clipboard nestling in his hand. Lovely you could make it, his expression seemed to suggest, I'm sure we're due for a lot of light-hearted fun.

It is customary for major stars to be preceded by a warm-up artiste, often a comedian, to encourage a bit of animation in their reactions. While Lord Young made a few last-minute adjustments to his overly-neat double-breasted suit, it fell to Lord St John of Fawsley to dust down an old gag or two. The DTI building, he drawled, was one of the most hid-e-ous structures in London, even in the Kingdom. Could it not now be demolished? Boom! Boom! The Government spokesman couldn't agree. Well, said Olde-Tyme trouper Lord "Uncle Bob" Mellish, if it wasn't the worst building, could he say what was worse? Boom! Boom!

By now, the House was beautifully warmed up, so much so that steam could be seen to rise from some of its most prominent members. Lord Young had finished wiping his spectacles and was now folding and refolding his handkerchief, ready to pop it back, crisp and clean, into his top pocket. He rose, stretched both arms out and prepared for his inquisition. In front of him sat his opposing panellists, all with their gongs to the fore.

Lord Shackleton said that he would not accuse Lord Young of mislead-ing the House, a trick statement really meaning that he would accuse Lord

Young of misleading the House. "I did not mislead Your Lordship's House", declared Lord Young. The position on the Radarsat project was very simple, he said: "We will make up our minds in good time". His bright, somewhat over-large white cuffs seemed to twinkle in the sunlight.

"I accept Lord Young's expression of regret that the House was undoubtedly misled", chipped in Lord Shackleton, who was fast revealing that his own knowledge of techniques employed on "Take Your Pick" was virtually encyclopaedic.

"Excuse me", Lord Young, his face reddening, his cuffs a-quiver, leapt to his feet. "Excuse me but I did not mislead the House. I stand by each and every word I said."

Lord Shackleton then seemed to say that he had not meant to say what he had said about what Lord Young had said he hadn't said, but then he ruined it by saying again what he hadn't meant to say. "Of course I withdraw that remark. I just hope the Noble Lord will come a bit cleaner", he said, adding: "It is within the knowledge of the House that the House was deceived".

By this time, the Conservative benches were banging their gongs, demanding that the temporary quizmaster be dismissed. Lord Young sat back, his ordeal over, his smile somewhat less avid than usual. And as for Lord Shackleton, he received the due punishment meted out to so many offenders in our society. Lord Longford sidled over and patted him on the back. *12 April 1988*

From which it may be inferred that Their Noble Lordships know their Place

FOR THE first half hour or so, Mr Nicholas Ridley sat on the bottom step of the Throne, one leg out, one leg in, scowling and uncomfortable, like a raddled old Christopher Robin whose Meths supply was in danger of being confiscated. His beloved Poll Tax was in danger of being amended into oblivion, and he could make no yelp or cry in its support.

Lord Chelwood was the first of the grown-ups to wish for its confiscation. He wears his moustache like a gentleman, and he orates like a gentleman too, which is to say that he makes such devoted use of pauses that the words which emerge are few and far between.

He spoke as if muttering over breakfast about a particularly disagreeable item on the Letters page of *The Times*. Occasionally, it seemed that during the pauses between grunts he might pop a fried egg into his mouth and wash it down with some lashings of luke-warm coffee. "I want", he said, "to say", he continued, "one thing", he went on, "that I find", he elaborated, "difficult to say". It emerged that he was a trifle miffed at the opposition to his amendment. In particular, he felt that the accusation that he had no right to change the bill was "uncalled for".

"And when er, erm, and when Wood, erm", he began, leaning over to get a prompt from a neighbour before continuing. "Yes, and when erm Lord Wyatt – I was going to say Woodrow – spoke of 'disembowelling ourselves' well, I really did think that that was a bit much."

Here was a man who had emerged wholly unscathed from the white hot heat of the technological revolution; not for him the crash-course in self-assertion or the week of seminars on how to be a TV personality. His every um and er, his every fumble at his hand-written and ill-sorted speech, his every "bit much" and "uncalled for" acted as a reassuring guarantee of his worth.

At losing his place, Lord Chelwood has no equal. "The actual quote is er um er. . .if I can find it", he said at one point, and, at another: "We promised in the last manifesto which I er might find er if I can er find it. . ." He eventually quoted Robert Burns, and referred to Wat Tyler ("came to a very sticky end") before turning the page on to his last paragraph. "My Lords", he said, "we are in a mess".

After Lord Chelwood, Lord Whitelaw seemed fast and flashy and fearfully modern, an extraordinary cross between Simon Dee and Captain Pugwash. Taking to the spirit of the Upper House like a duck to water, his attacks are all prefaced by compliments. "My Noble Lord Chelwood, whom I greatly admire and whom I do not seek to criticize", he began, in the manner of one cheerily offering a cigarette and asking: "Are you sitting comfortably?" before switching on the electric chair.

"I do not seek to criticize": were Lord Whitelaw ever to take the plunge and start to criticize, the whole House would very quickly be in tears. He declared that the arguments against the Community Charge "are not well thought out, indeed, they don't seem to be thought out at all". He favours adages that might have been plundered from one of Baden-Powell's discarded notebooks, or from a half-remembered motto off *Blue Peter*. "Every man should be judged by the company he keeps", he declared, peering at the Labour benches as if surveying the most miserable band of loafers and ne'er-do-wells. Lord Callaghan smiled back.

He addressed the Upper House under the obvious belief that it was formed entirely of well-meaning but dim-witted cooks. "If that is what the House decides to do that is what the House will do and I will stand up for it but I believe it will bitterly regret its decision", he said. In another life, he would have made an admirable Nanny, always called back from retirement by fretting mothers with unmanageable infants. With one "because I say so" he could silence the most disruptive nursery.

Eyebrows raised in perpetual bemusement that no-one is ever quite as clever as him, Lord Hailsham rose to scoff at notions of "ability to pay". With his characteristic knowing smirk, he declared that "ability to pay is as long as a piece of string". But by this time Christopher Robin had exited, determined never ever to trust in grown-ups again. *24 March 1988*

8

THE END OF THE

THE

ALLIANCE

Containing many Mishaps

Containing the Strong Promise of reconciliation after an Election Defeat and Harsh Words

NORTHERN Ireland Questions never sees the House at its most full, though one or two members can be spotted from time to time. Mr Tom King, the Secretary of State for Northern Ireland, has a high attendance record, though he might well investigate the saving involved in sending a tape-recording of his previous statements in his place.

Most of his sentences include at least two of the following words: "welcoming", "very real", "opportunity", "assurance", "co-operation" or "encouraging". Such nice words occur in the House only when the situation they are describing is nasty.

"Continuing to yield encouraging results", Mr King said, as the time ticked by. Unionist members attempted a heckle or two, but without much enthusiasm.

Mr Ian Paisley, often such a lively contributor, was rumoured to have already left for his holiday, so perhaps the vision of that Reverend gentleman, alcohol-free lager in hand, trouser-legs rolled up, hankie on head, merrily whizzing along on his windsurfer was arousing sufficient envy among his confederates to subdue their fiercer passion.

Questions to the Prime Minister were beginning at 3.15pm, so the three hundred or so members who rolled in at 3.14pm had the opportunity to listen to a good fifty seconds or so of spirited discussion on Northern Ireland. As talk turned to the dangers of too rigid sectarianism, Dr David Owen came in, followed closely by Mr David Steel.

It has been some time now since these two opposing factions have been seen together in public. When Mr Steel chose to sit next to Dr Owen, many observers felt that a welcome opportunity for the assurance of encouraging closer co-operation had become very real.

While Mr King moved finally to plastic bullets, Mr Steel turned to Dr Owen and began to talk with some animation. Dr Owen, in his legs-stretched, arms-folded, sun-worshipping posture, looked outwards, as if grudgingly listening to the hypochondriacal gibberish of a malingering fatality.

"Questions to the Prime Minister!" announced the Speaker, and Mrs Thatcher in blue suit with navy trimmings, took up her place by the Despatch Box. It was now Dr Owen's turn to speak to Mr Steel. Tomorrow, they would be off on holiday: could they kiss and make up before parting? The House was on tenterhooks, so much so that even when their Leader was speaking of the Common Agricultural Policy, many Conservatives found their eyes straying to the couple opposite.

Dr Owen was telling a joke to Mr Steel. After what seemed like years, Mr Steel smiled. Ah! Everyone felt so happy for them, so very happy. Mr Steel then stood up to leave for the Liberal bench. "He's going now!" shouted Mr Dennis Skinner in his ribald cackle. Some people can be so coarse.

Not wishing to intrude, the Prime Minister carried on talking about the Common Agricultural Policy. Dr Owen, in his black, black suit sought consolation with Mrs Rosie Barnes, whose crisp cotton blouse was so clean that it had an almost bluey whiteness.

"Why doesn't she have the guts to tell it to the House of Commons?" spluttered Mr Roy Hattersley about something-or-other. "Why doesn't he have the guts to accept precisely what happened?" trilled the Prime Minister in return.

Mr Steel smiled softly to himself. Squabbles were so unnecessary. Mr Gerald Kaufman heckled the Prime Minister but the Prime Minister brushed him off with ease, in a scene strangely reminiscent of the Tom and Jerry cartoon series in which the large lady with the broom gets rid of little Jerry with one fell sweep.

But as Mr Steel smiled, Dr Owen began listening intently to Mr John Cartwright (SDP), as if he had forgotten all about that happy moment he had just shared with the Liberal leader. Would Cartwright win Owen back? Would Steel leave Owen – forever! Who knows? That was the final episode in the present series. A new series begins at the SDP conference in September.

24 July 1987

In which Mr Maclennan steps out of the Chorus, involving impressive hand-gestures

"I'LL JUST give you one example", said John during the course of the Looking Forward to the 1990s debate. But as he said it, the amber light on the rostrum changed to red. "I don't think there's time actually John", interrupted Mr William Rodgers from above. And so John withdrew, taking his one example with him.

Watching the light change from green to amber and then to red has been one of the most rewarding activities offered by the SDP conference in Portsmouth. As each speaker arrives at the dais, the light goes green. After a couple of minutes it turns to amber, and the speaker begins to speak very fast. It is around this time that the speaker decides to expand his original point – on, perhaps, the future of the antimergerites in Chiswick northwest – to a more general discussion on the future of the world.

And then the light goes red and they toddle back to their seats.

Once in a long while, a famous SDP member speaks and the Gods seem to lean forward for a few seconds from their pillows. A couple of weeks ago, Mr Robert Maclennan might easily have dressed up as Widow Twankey and waltzed his way around the Palace of Westminster and no-one would have noticed. These days, his presence in a room is enough for experts to declare that room not entirely empty.

His presence on the platform yesterday even brought people to their feet, and not merely to look for him under their chairs. Looking like the photographic model in a seaside barber's shop, he strode confidently to the platform to make what pundits had called the most difficult speech of his life.

As difficult speeches go, it was pretty easy. As soon as he entered, Dr David Owen gave him a pat on the back, a photogenic thumbs-up and a standing ovation. Mrs Shirley Williams then recommended his courage, determination and integrity.

His stage act is quite obviously strongly influenced by the slightly famous sixties pop group Reparata and the Delrons who almost reached the Top Ten in the mid-to-late sixties with their hit record "Something Here in My Heart".

The chorus went, you will remember, "Something here-here-here in my heart keeps a-tellin' me no", and as Reparata enunciated the words "here-here-here" she would move her hands towards her heart and then back into the air, in a manner owing more to rehearsal than instinct.

He kicked off his speech with a joke or two. A joke from Mr Maclennan can be identified by the short pause that immediately follows it. He had read in the press, he said, that he was "a dapper dresser" and, he continued, "although delighted by all of this, my tailor does not seriously expect that I am about to do for his business prospects what her Royal Highness the

Princess of Wales achieved for the Emanuels". A laugh swept through the conference hall as a drip of water might sweep through the Kalahari.

Mr Maclennan then got down to some serious gesticulation. "June, as we all know, was not good enough." This was the hard-hitting stuff the conference had been waiting for. ". . .today, the raging must stop. The realism starts here!" As the word "here" emerged from Maclennan's mouth, his right hand made a weird flamboyant gesture towards the ground. The man who had believed himself to be a Delron for life was proving himself a worthy Reparata.

"If the time is right for union then you will know and so will I." Brave words indeed, and made all the more courageous by the waving of an arm in the air.

"We owe it to ourselves. . ." he went on, his hands now coming together to point at his body. . ."We owe it to the British electorate. . ." and the hands, now out of control, began summoning a waiter. ". . .that is what my leadership is all about". And with that, he sat down.

They stood and they clapped and they cheered and Dr Owen did another thumbs up. They remained standing as long as they could, perhaps worried that if they sat down he might ask them what he had said.

2 September 1987

∞∞∞

In which the Sketchwriter chances upon a Major Document

NOT FOR *publication before the end of the period immediately prior to publication.*
The basis upon which the constitution of the data upon which the amendments to the structures upon which the Social Democratic Party and the Liberal Party are to join to form a new political party, to be known hereinafter as EITHER the Social Democratic and Liberal Party OR the Liberal and Social Democratic Party OR the Liberatic and Demi-Social Party OR none of the above are outlined in the following joint document, agreed in a meeting between representatives of all or both the above parties, and countersigned by a substantial minority.

1. This Assembly recognizes the need for a new political party roughly the same as the existing two but without Dr David Owen this time.

2. The new political party will be founded on a commitment to individual freedom, social justice, responsible stewardship of the earth and its resources and a committed distrust of Dr David Owen.

3. To this end, it will continue to speak of Dr David Owen in terms of the warmest regard but only when he is in the room. It will further nurture the

realistic idea that the major steps forward in the last six years of the Social Democratic Party came about as a direct result of the charisma and forceful personality of Mr Bob Maclennan who is the one with the neat hair you hadn't heard of until a couple of weeks ago, you know, yes, that one.

4. The new political party will be open, democratic and participatory for all who have achieved, through sheer dint of talent and hard work, a senior position in the hierarchy. It will be innovative, exciting and revolutionary.

5. To this end, Mrs Shirley Williams, Mr David Steel, Mr Bill Rodgers and Mr Alan Beith will all hold senior posts.

6. The new political party will hold regular assemblies wherein all delegates will have the opportunity to debate animal rights, gun control, raffia work and anti-smoking legislation at great length but only in the late afternoon period when anyone remotely influential has cleared off.

7. The formation of the new party should involve free training schemes and summer schools to aid the recognition of jokes and serious statements by Mr Bob Maclennan and distinguish the difference between the two. Further courses in Related Laughter will be provided for those on the platform likely to be caught by the cameras. Sentences by Mr Maclennan which begin, "I stand before you today as Leader of the SDP. . ." are generally not intended for merriment.

8. In accordance with amendment XII para (e), all speaking delegates will be required to offer three adjectives – eg, tired, exhausted, worn out – when one would be enough, sufficient, necessary.

9. Members having a common interest may organize in autonomous groups with a defined procedure for recognition so that those who hold views contradictory to those of others might still be able to define themselves as belonging to the same party.

10. In the interests of party unity, members will include the words Thatcher and Hard Left in all speeches, coupled always with one from the selection of adjectives in amendment XIV para 7 incl. crippling, divisive, uncaring, ruthless, undemocratic.

11. Policy is of prime importance in the formation of the new party. It will be broadly-based, attractive and agreeable to all the people of this country and not just one particular sector. In the interests of national unity, policy will include arguments both for and against. Thus policy (a) will be followed by the words "but on the other hand" introducing policy (b) stating the opposing view. Members will be free to choose which they prefer, or neither, or both, or, in exceptional circumstances, neither and both.

12. The party structure will be revolutionary and mould-breaking. Regional committees will elect national committees which will elect consultative committees which will elect selection committees which will elect regional committees.

13. Apart from the above, business as usual.   *17 September 1987*

Containing the promise of great Happiness arising from The Liberal Assembly

"**I** WANT the press to leave this assembly and transmit the wonderful message of hope", said a female delegate. She looked forward to the "wonderful and marvellous mountains for us to scale and conquer" and felt that, "at the end of the day, there is a lot of love in this party".

There were strong hints of a Country and Western song lurking, ready to pounce. This song would, no doubt, be played over the sparkling amplifiers at the event that had been planned all week: the marvellous new party.

But what sort of party will it be and will anyone want to come? Certainly there are some in the street who do not want a new party at all, and if they come they will be determined to make it bring-a-battle.

Even the drafting of the invitation was enough to put some people off the whole idea. "In line five, after the word 'which' insert the word 'commitment'" said smoothie Colin Darracot, chairman-for-a-day. "Also put a semi-colon after the bracket." It was hardly the stuff of "Hey, guys, let's have the party right here!" so beloved of movie funsters.

There were some who did not approve of the invitation to the invitation to the invitation to the party. "There's no mention of a party which looks forward to peace", said one delegate. Nor was there any mention of a party committed to being as nice as possible for most of the time, but sooner or later someone was bound to suggest it. "There's not a single word about it being a party that is not just pluralist, decentralized, and open but also activist", said another.

But almost everyone was agreed that the old party had run its course. All the great party characters whose names were evoked – "This is the party of Lloyd George, Gladstone and Asquith" – had left long ago, and that the man who was now greeting guests, a Mr David Steel, was more of a gifted washer-up than a host in the grand tradition.

Nevertheless, it seemed impolite to abandon the old party without first depositing a bread-and-butter letter on the mantelpiece. But somehow it never rings quite true if excessive thanks are delivered as one hot-foots it next door.

"We are a great movement", said Mr Tim Clement Jones, waving ta-ra. He then delivered a succession of compliments. "Liberals have never been backward-looking", he said. Others delivered their thanks in a less straight-forward way. "We are a bottom-up party", said another delegate, perhaps harking back to the mid-seventies. "Not just a party for today but a party of tomorrow."

But the invitation to tomorrow's party still seemed a little ill-defined. A young man in glasses said that it should be a "third world party", and a young girl said that it should be a party to "reach out to young people and appeal to people at all levels".

Mr Tony Greave, who normally favours bean-bag parties in which partygoers gather in the kitchen to criticize their hosts, seemed to have changed his tune. "Liberals want a party we can be happy in", he said. For him, this was a major change of personal policy: for years he has favoured being as disgruntled as possible. Invited to a wine-and-cheese party, he would complain of the lack of lager and chocolate cookies; invited to a pyjama party he would turn up in morning suit. But today he was on best behaviour.

Good as the old party had been, no-one seemed, as they waved their drunken goodbyes, to remember quite what had gone on at it. A young and thrusting man declared that it had never been a unilateralist party. "Rubbish!", came a scream from the audience. "We are not narrow partisans", said someone else. Somewhere, the Federation of Narrow Partisan Liberals was tabling a motion to dissociate itself from the remarks of the previous speaker.

As they run out of the old party into the night, leaving a few stragglers behind them, they seem sure in their own minds that the next party will be better, better, better. They love a party with a happy atmosphere. And that, within its limits, is a marvellous message of hope.   *18 September 1987*

∞∞∞

In which the Sketchwriter travels to Sheffield to witness the beginning of a Great Adventure

"LET ME ask you to rise with me and welcome David Owen." Mr John Cartwright, ever the greeter in a prosperous firm of undertakers, had been judged the man most fitted to make the speech of welcome.

In marched Dr Owen, waving his assured and manly wave. Taking to the rostrum – a set in front of the official set, strangely reminiscent of a Punch and Judy box plopped into the middle of the Royal Opera House – he held raised hands with John and Rosie, his crocodile smile snapping around in search of babies to eat.

"I think that says it all" he said, as the applause died down. He stood erect and immobile, his hands on the edge of the dais, black hair, white cuffs, dark suit, red eyes. Rosie, dressed in prim black and beaming away like Mary Poppins gone loopy, stared wide-eyed up at the Doctor from her seat. This is a man, she seemed to be thinking, for whom I would gladly be Chancellor of the Exchequer.

[106]

"Remember how they used to write about us – that we were a rump, a faction, a fan-club" continued Dr Owen to his rump, his faction, his fan-club. Mary Poppins's eyes seemed to mist over at the memory. If need be, she would be his Foreign Secretary and his Minister of Trade as well.

The Doctor praised the courage and conviction, the tremendous clarity and consistency, of those who still agreed with him. "We all sustained each other," he declared. "We who love this party – and there are many in this room who love this party," he went on, and Mary Poppins continued to beam upwards, now sure in the knowledge that she would, if called upon, take on the portfolios of Health, Employment and Northern Ireland, "We who *love* this party – we will not be forced into a loveless marriage."

This was a sombre Doctor, barely raising his voice, his once-dangling forelock now cut and trimmed and neatly swept back. Many of his old gestures had been abandoned: no more the "when I was Foreign Secretary", no more the uplift on the end of each paragraph to indicate a suitable period for applause, no more the purposeful gesticulations or the shrewd half-smiles.

This was the International Statesman, above all that. "There's no need to cut each others' throats as we go our separate ways," he stated, the director of the abattoir espousing the noble cause of lifelong vegeterianism.

Perhaps quoting from Peter Pan, he began to talk of the "Great Adventure" on which they had embarked. "You've got to know what you love and fight for what you love".

Oh, yes! Oh, yes! Her smile all a-quiver, Mary Poppins seemed about to burst into song. *Chim-chimenee, chim-chimenee, chim-chim-cheroo. Good luck will rub off when I shake hands with you.* Those joyous words kept flooding back.

For Mr Maclennan's speech the next day, Mary Poppins stood at one side, her side smile now absent. At the last SDP conference, Poor Bob's freshly-choreographed gesticulations lent him the appearance of a well-to-do Catherine Wheel, but now he, too, was sombre, his curious twitchings more appropriate to a confrontation with a lackadaisical flea than with a mass rally of over-heating Social Democrats.

In moments of great seriousness, he bears a strong physical resemblance to a ventriloquist's dummy, his eyebrows leaping up and down on his forehead, his hair so carefully coiffed that it might be sculpted in plasticene, the words he enunciates sounding as if thrown from a little man – or possibly woman – crouched in the dais beneath him. He pronounces the word "found" to rhyme with "rind" and the "u" in "illusion" is borrowed from the word "Tuesday".

"I commend it to you: your vote must be yes." Mr Maclennan sat down and, rightly guessing that his speech must now be over, the audience stood up. Waving like a man who had only recently learnt how, Poor Bob issued a mouthy smile. The beams on the faces of the pro- and anti-mergerites as they left the hall made it clear that for them all, bliss was it in that dusk to be alive.

1 February 1988

⚬⚬

Introducing a New Party, a new future and some Old Faces

STARTING at 10.00 am, it looked much like one of television's new mid-morning panel games. On the raised platform to the left were the Members of Parliament. On the raised platform to the right were assorted unelected others. In the middle was a democracy of quizmasters, with Bob and Shirley and David to the fore. The name of the game, emblazoned behind them on a sort of golden-yellowish-orange colour, was "Social and Liberal Democrats: The New Choice, The Best Future".

This is the sort of title that has earned these panel games their special elevenses slot. They favour the less well known type of celebrity, the sort whose face rings a bell, but it is hard to remember quite why. Was he on a coffee advertisement four years ago or was he something to do with Max Bygraves, or was he once a ventriloquist, or is he now, perhaps, a Liberal MP? Maybe this will pioneer a whole new genre of quizgame, in which the audience has to guess exactly who each celebrity is.

The chief quizmaster took to the rostrum. He was Ian Wrigglesworth. Wasn't he the one who. . .no, no, that was someone else. "It is with a sense of relief and excitement that we come here today", he said, and, a minute later, he said: "It is with a sense of relief and excitement that we come here today". The other key phrase (10 points) was "a great sense of optimism". Everyone on the platform, it seemed, however glum they might have looked, was full of a great sense of optimism.

Ian asked the viewers to welcome Adrian. Adrian, he announced, represented "all that is best in the Liberal Party". Adrian said that he felt a strong sense of optimism. He talked of turning back the tide. "Thank you very much, Adrian", said Ian.

Next Ian invited on someone who had made "a major impact on the House of Commons and British politics since he was elected in 1983". Who could it be? Aha! It was a trick question! It was Mr Charles Kennedy, MP for Ross, Cromarty and Skye. Charles said a few words. Thank you very much, Charles.

Next came Geraint from Wales whose ambition is to be in Government by the turn of the century. "There's an excellent team behind me here. Give them a chance! That is the appeal from the people of Wales". (One of the more onerous aspects of being a politician from Wales seems to be that you can never be a single person: you must always be an entire people). Thank you, Geraint.

The next contestant had shown "great dignity and integrity", said Ian. Who could it be? Step forward, Robert Maclennan MP. His starter for 10: what was the purpose of the new party? "Our purpose is to revive and strengthen the effectiveness of democracy in Britain". Thank you very much, Bob.

And on to the next contestant, who had shown "great courage and determination". Welcome, David Steel. How are you feeling, David? "It is exhilarating to be here". And what do you intend to do? "We intend to give hope to a whole new generation". David made a joke about Lloyd George, and his fellow panellists put on their long, lingering, platform smiles to show they had got it. What sort of party are you, David? "We are a big party". Thank you, David, thank you.

Now there's a face we recognize! Shirley something. The one with the hair, you know. Used to be on television during elections. Ian introduced her: "Shirley has brought warmth and sincerity and understanding to British politics". Yes, that's the one – Shirley Williams! I knew she'd done something like that. So what do you want for your country, Shirley? "We want for our country the best of futures". Thank you very much, Shirley.

So those were the panellists: now what about the prizes? But the game is not yet over! The gentlemen of the Press can ask some questions. There are one or two questions about Dr Owen ("insignificant splinter, insignificant splinter") but no-one can think of anything else to ask.

And so the prize is wheeled on. The chance to sign the Founders' Book! See them queue, all with their shiny gold pens! Welcome, as the brochure says, to the Social and Liberal Democrats.   *4 March 1988*

Being a Brief survey of the Power and Influence of the Social and Liberal Democrats

ODDLY enough, Mr Alan Beith already has a job of national standing. He is the Honourable Member answering for the House of Commons Commission.

This post entitles him to: a) a large, brown, lightweight, cardboard folder; b) five minutes every few weeks answering questions from members of all parties on the internal running of the House of Commons. Not a paperclip can be ordered into service in the House of Commons without first being subjected to the scrutiny of Mr Beith.

From the point of view of all the other members of the SLD and the SDP, this makes Mr Beith a powerbroker of quite extraordinary influence, but this Henry Kissinger of the moderate classes wears his grandeur with modesty.

Though he dresses in a double-breasted suit, Mr Beith is not what you would call a double-breasted sort of person. He is more the helpful man behind the counter at the corner-shop with the biro protruding from the top pocket of his overalls, or the village deacon who enjoys a bit of train-spotting when he can find the time. Mildness is his middle name.

This month's five minutes of Mr Beith occurred between 3.15 and 3.20 yesterday afternoon. It was, as usual, extremely mild. Mr Graham Allen, a spikey-faced new Labour MP, much given to worrying about this, that and the other, requested the appointment of a full-time officer to be in charge of all public tickets and tours around the House. As if this were not enough, he also wanted "facilities for basic shopping purposes" for "the increasing number of members who work full-time in the House".

Well, it might not yet be Supreme Power, but it's a start. Mr Beith brought out his large, brown, lightweight cardboard folder, flourishing this trapping of office with visible pride. Yes, he would look into the first matter, but he thought that the question of a supermarket on the premises was "a question which goes much wider".

Next up was Mr Tony Banks, who always seems to be up, ever ready with a cocksure crack and a loopy distress signal. Now, he wanted to worry about the unpleasant working conditions for the staff of the Palace of Westminster, and, after jokes – stop it, it's hurting – about hot air, he complained that it was "one of the smelliest, sweatiest workplaces" in the land and "should not be tolerated".

Mr Beith must have been tempted to blame it all on that pushy Mr Ashdown, always leaping up and down stairs two-at-a-time in his shirt-sleeves, working up a fair old sweat. But he refrained. They had spent three-quarters of a million pounds on air conditioning in the kitchen, he said, adding, without even a glance at Mr Ashdown's empty seat, that more work was still needed.

Let us leave Mr Beith, now sedentary, cradling his large, brown, light-weight cardboard folder in his arms, a satisfied smile playing on his lips after a job well done, and turn to the next act, Mr John Wakeham, who seems overly laden with titles and posts. Normally Leader of the House, he was now answering questions as Lord President of the Council. What more could a man want?

But every robe of office has its moth, and no moth comes more persistent in its flapping than Mr Tam Dalyell. Mr Dalyell combines long-windedness with obscurantism, so it is often tricky to catch his drift, but he seemed to have been reading Mr Julian Critchley's biography of Michael Hesltine, and had dug from it further revelations on Westland. Of course, Mr Dalyell is capable of finding references to Westland in *Anne of Green Gables*, but still Mr Wakeham felt obliged to answer.

He had read the Heseltine biography, he revealed, while waiting for his son to be born last autumn, and he had nothing further to say. The House allowed this bizarre comment to pass without muster, but what sort of a man chooses to plough through a biography of Michael Heseltine while his wife is giving birth to their baby?

The heights of political life do strange and terrible things to a human being. Mr Alan Beith should learn from this awful lesson and cast aside his large, brown, lightweight cardboard folder before it is too late.

28 June 1988

In which the Sketchwriter travels to Kensington to witness Fierce Exchanges between Old Friends in pursuit of By-election Victory

WHAT a marvellous word is "satisfactory" and how under-used it is outside the schoolroom. It covers a universe of meanings, yet is only employed when things are not quite what was hoped for. "Satisfactory" on a school report is only ever used to describe marks somewhat under five out of 10, yet its air of competence saves many a child the rod. Yesterday it enjoyed a most heartening revival in the SLD and SDP morning press conferences for the Kensington by-election.

By and large, the press believe that both parties, now such bitter enemies, are way on course for disastrous results tomorrow. In their hearts, both parties seem to know this too. This is where the word "satisfactory" comes in. Asked his predictions for the SLD result, Mr Charles Kennedy declared: "We will come out with a very satisfactory result."

Mr Robert Maclennan seemed to think likewise. "I anticipate we'll do much better in this by-election than had been forecast before we began," he said.

"I agree with what Bob has just said," chipped in Mr David Steel. ". . .I hope very much this by-election will provide the springboard for our new leader."

Now, this was hardly quite as uproarious a response to events as his demand a year or two ago for those within earshot to go back to their constituencies and prepare for Government. He had probably decided that "Stay in your constituency and prepare for humiliation" would not have quite the same ring to it.

Nevertheless, a strange atmosphere of jollity pervaded both the SLD and the SDP press conferences. This seemed to be due to the fact that each thought the other was doing even worse. Mr Kennedy unveiled his party's latest returns with undisguised glee. They put the Conservatives at 48 per cent, Labour at 26 per cent, the SLD at 20 per cent and – tarantara! tarantara! – "Dr Owen's party" at 3 per cent. Yippee! Mr Maclennan put on his finest man-of-infinite-depths smile, which he assumes makes him look like the Mona Lisa, but in fact makes him look rather more like that versatile glove-puppet Sweep. "I think the 3 per cent could be described as statistically insignificant," he squeaked.

Down the hill at the SDP, Rosie Barnes and Dr Owen seemed to think that everything was going rather more, er, satisfactorily for them. "In some areas we're fairly clear we've been able to win some support that was not there before," said the doctor. He has now become so addicted to giving the let's-not-get-too-carried-away view of things that he applies it rather over-readily to his party's own prospects, failing to muster much optimism. "Wouldn't it be a tremendous humiliation to lose your deposit?" asked a journalist. "That depends on the results," replied Dr Owen. Only a few days before, his candidate, John Martin, had been determinedly declaring that he was aiming to win.

But Dr Owen still managed to take heart from what he had seen. "We are now beginning to see the identity of the party that I hoped would emerge in 1981," he declared. Looking at the identity of the party on show – the odd, doll-like figure of Rosie Barnes, her face now absurdly over-animated, now as sullen as a waxwork, alongside the heavily bespectacled, know-it-all face of Mr Martin – it seemed a most bizarre hope, and one scarcely worth waiting a full seven years to see realized.

Dr Owen spends much of his time and energy in not attacking his former colleagues. Instead, he points out that they are spending a lot of their time attacking him, and doesn't that tell you all you'd want to know about the kind of people they are? Mr Martin favours the more direct approach. When Dr Owen was asked to comment on a recent claim to the roots of Social Democracy from Lord Jenkins of Hillhead, Mr Martin stepped in. "Arrant nonsense," he said, reminding the press of the days Dick Taverne had spent waiting for "his friend and colleague Roy Jenkins" to appear at his by-election, "and he waited in vain". And what could be less satisfactory than that?   *13 July 1988*

The SLD came third with 10.7%, the SDP fourth with 5%.

∞

Containing a New Leader, some Christian names and a Cleaner from Crossroads Motel

AN UNUSUAL number of people had gathered outside the Social and Liberal Democratic Party headquarters. Towards the centre of the front door stood Mr Paddy Ashdown, his slit eyes surveying some distant horizon, his lips pursed in a half-smile. Standing on a lower step, rather off-centre, was Mr Alan Beith, orange tie and orange rose at the ready, smiling great big smiles in sporadic bursts.

How speedily politicians resume their insignificance! Somewhere behind both of them stood Mr David Steel, fresh from a farewell lunch. "Wasn't he the one who. . .?" passers-by seemed to be asking themselves, before coming up with the answer, "Yes, that's it, he once had his own quiz-show, oooh, years ago".

Mr Ian Wrigglesworth had just been declared president. He, like every-one else, had a vision for the future. What he wanted to see was "not the SDP nor the Liberal Party but a new party forged of the two old parties". A bronzed Mrs Shirley Williams – didn't she used to clean the chalets in Crossroads motel? – read out the figures for the leadership election, conclud-ing: "I therefore declare Paddy Ashdown elected as leader of the Social and Liberal Democrats". There was a sprinkle of applause of a modesty befitting an audience composed mainly of journalists.

"I say to the millions out there" began Mr Ashdown, "who care about poverty and unemployment – come and join us". He then gave an inventory of things worth caring about – environment, peaceful world, better world, and so on – interspersing each section with the chant "come and join us". The dual ability to say "come and join us" while squinting into the distance seemed, to his supporters around the doorway, further proof of Mr Ash-down's charisma. "The Social and Liberal Democrats are about building a better future – and we start today!" he boomed.

Inside the party headquarters, posters from the leadership and presiden-tial campaigns still hung on the walls, all with headlines of hopes for the new party.

"We Must Win The Battle For Ideas", said Mr Ashdown's poster. "Clarity and Depth Will Help Us Win" said Mr Beith's. "The Man To Turn To In a Crisis" said Mr Des Wilson's.

At his press conference indoors, Mr Ashdown launched his first salvo in the battle for ideas. Our party was progressively defined as a) "An open and debating party" b) "a participative party" c) "a party that remembers we can't attack Mrs Thatcher by defending the past" d) "a party distinct and different". But asked for more specific definitions, he grew somewhat bad-tempered.

Noting Mr Ashdown's edginess and aggression in victory, onlookers could only shudder to imagine what he would have been like in defeat. "What d'you expect me to say?" "Oh, come on! – " these were the sort of comments that preceded his rather more public statements of the "I think the party is in a mood to go forward" type.

He is a keen user of the Christian name. "Yes, Mike – ". "Well, John". He likes to inject an air of certainty into his battle for ideas by preceding most of his statements with the words "I have no doubt whatsoever". If ever he were to entertain doubts, he would most likely reply along the lines of "I have no doubt whatsoever, Mike, that our new party, being an open and participative party, distinct and different, must go forward if it does not wish to go back, and must certainly not go back if it wishes to go forward, and – let me say this without the shadow of a doubt, John – there are real and positive advantages in not having a clue, particularly when you have a party of such outstanding calibre as I know from my own experience we have".

But in the most important area of SLD philosophy, the distinct, open and participative loathing of Dr David Owen, he had no doubt where he stands. "You treat irrelevancies as people you don't pay much attention to" he said, his head jutting forward, his eyes squidging up, his half-smile coming and going with the speed of a swift and shiny knife.   *26 July 1988*

9
RIVALS

In which Mr Benn's instructions to Concentrate on Issues are Strictly Observed, but with small success

Containing a difference of opinion between Mr John Prescott and Mr Cecil Parkinson

MR JOHN Prescott is not one of nature's frailer flowers. Were he ever to come close to a tulip he would probably bite its head off, keeping the stalk as a truncheon for pesky butterflies. Burly and greasy-haired, he looks rather like one of those plain-talking policemen who, during the late 1970s, were always being photographed on yachting holidays with villains somewhere in the Mediterranean.

It was Mr Prescott, you will remember, who turned upon the then Sir James Callaghan as he was enjoying a teacake in the House of Commons tearoom, and it was Mr Prescott again who was set to oust Mr Roy Hattersley from the deputy leadership of the Labour Party. Any well-adjusted man of reasonable build will, at some time in his life, have been tempted into one or both of these acts, but it takes one of Mr Prescott's ilk to come so close to carrying them off.

Observers of Parliament are often drawn to the school metaphor: so-and-so is the sneak, so-and-so the headmaster, so-and-so the swot. For an accurate description of Mr Prescott, one would have to leave the school, march through the playground and there, standing at the school gate, a janitor's cap sitting proudly on his head, would be Mr Prescott.

He is Labour's spokesman for energy, the opposite number to Mr Cecil Parkinson. They are an unlikely couple, the rough and the smooth, or even the chalk and the cheese, though it would be hard to find a chalk sufficiently tough, or a cheese sufficiently gooey.

Mr Parkinson donned spectacles to read a statement announcing his plans to privatize the electricity industry. He thought it would make the industry marvellously go-ahead and modern and competitive, but those who have had experience of the privatization of the telephone system will be rather more worried. When the customer presses a light switch, will the light take 10 minutes to come on, and then only in the wrong room? Those are the sort of worries faced by the consumer, and it was for Mr Prescott to voice them.

It was the triumph of ideology over commonsense, he said. It was all about the exploitation of the consumer. It took the electricity supply industry back 50 years. It had absolutely nothing to do with competition. Mr Prescott delivered these complaints in a tone that went from aggressive to very aggressive via rather too aggressive.

Observers found it hard to tell how Mr Parkinson was reacting to such coarseness. His mouth twitched, his head jerked and his eyes shifted around, but they do that all the time anyway. As Mr Prescott punched and banged his way through a litany of absolute disgraces and downright exploitations, the more uncouth among the Conservatives began to grow restless, so that the noise in the chamber began to sound something like this: "Absolute Yarawayhay Disgrace Baroompapah Downright Chirpycheepcheep Disgrace Lalalabamba".

Mr Prescott began to grow tetchy, unusually so for a man who looks as if he spent his youth arm-wrestling mechanical diggers in dimly-lit basement bars. His "absolutes" and his "disgraces" grew ever more vehement, but the Tories yahooed all the more. Eventually, sweat creeping on to his brow, he could stand it no longer. He turned to the Speaker. "I must protest", he spluttered furiously, "at the barracking of the yobboes on that side!"

Oh, how they laughed! "Yahahahahahahaha. Yahahahahahaha". Mr Geoffrey Dickens, little arms reaching around a vast stomach, rolled to and fro in his seat like a child's dolly. A keen barracker, the extravagantly Brylcreemed Mr Dickens was delighted by this compliment from an opponent he obviously regards as his barracking superior. "Yahahahahaha! Yahahahahaha!"

"In conclusion, Mr Speaker", continued Mr Prescott, and the Tories hooted afresh. Mr Prescott stood still for a second and, in silence, pointed a finger and gave a threatening jab of his head. Had the hooters been eating teacakes, he might have shoved them in their faces. But as they were not, he returned to his speech. Phew.   *26 February 1988*

In which Mr John Prescott makes another Appearance, on this Occasion with a view to taking Mr Roy Hattersley's job

WERE he ever to become the feast and not the feaster, Mr Roy Hattersley might discover that his lower lip could make a perfectly substantial main course in its own right. By no means petite, and with a lumbering life all of its own, this lower lip carries much of Mr Hattersley's political conviction on, as it were, its shoulders. While the body so cumbersomely adjoined to it lies slumped in its seat, the lower lip, protruding away, is expected to signal all types of disapproval at the government policy of the day.

Yesterday, it was hard at work expressing its dissatisfaction with Mr Douglas Hurd's statement on overcrowding in prisons. As Mr Hurd barked his way through a series of fourthlys and fifthlys on what he was going to do with all those prisoners, Mr Hattersley could be seen staring over his gold-rimmed spectacles, fumbling through a pile of papers.

When his turn came to reply, he plopped himself in front of the Despatch Box and, pressing his pudgy finger into the air, proceeded to speak in his characteristic style, turning sentences back to front in the mistaken belief that it lends them solemnity, spluttering out an inventory of indignant adverbs.

"The Home Shecretary hash been far lesh than candid," he began, and the Tories seemed unwilling to raise a heckle, preferring to nod off gently, as if listening to a repeat broadcast on the Home Service. "Hish reshponsh to the crishish ish wholly inadequate," he continued, the full weight of his body now pressed horribly against the Despatch Box. He plopped back into his seat, placing his spectacles in his upper pocket, obviously believing himself to be Mr Robert Donat playing The Man Who Speaks the Truth, but more closely resembling Mr Terry Scott in one of his less energetic kitchen romps.

Mr Douglas Hurd seemed unaffected by Mr Hattersley's derision. Mr Hattersley would obviously know about overcrowding, he said, given the state of the current deputy leadership contest. Ho, ho, ho, went the Tories.

Again, Mr Hattersley's lower lip sprung to its master's defence, protruding itself menacingly in the direction of the Home Secretary. Meanwhile, in the Jubilee Room of the Palace of Westminster, one of Mr Hattersley's overcrowders, Mr John Prescott, was getting ready for a press conference.

Mr Prescott has the quick smile and bluff air of the croupier in a lunchtime casino in a run-down seaside resort. His cheery grin seems to be saying "Don't mess around with me, matey", before disappearing back into its stubbly frame.

He appeared with a merry little moustachioed MP, Mr Peter Snape. They sat down together, John poured himself a glass of water, Peter said, "John Prescott will read out a prepared statement – John", and John read out his prepared statement.

John is not a terrific reader, leaving over-long pauses between each word, as if rehearsing the next in his head before committing it to the sound waves. ". . . and . . . the . . . political . . . choice . . . that . . . I . . . will . . . offer . . . to . . . the . . . party . . . will . . . strengthen . . . Neil's . . . leadership," his statement concluded. "Any questions?" said Peter.

He didn't accept that for one moment, no, he didn't accept that for one moment. This was the gist of his comments to the press. He wished to encourage debate. Yes, he would win. No, he didn't think it would be fair to make comment on any past deputy leader. No, he didn't want to spell out any differences. No, he couldn't say how many unions were backing him.

How his memory must have travelled back to his days as a steward on passenger ships in the Merchant Navy! No, the cafeteria is not open, no, I don't know when it will be open, yes, it will open some time, no, I won't tell you when, yes, I'm thoroughly delighted to be encouraging such a demo-cratic debate.

Mr Snape had announced at the beginning that they were very sorry but John could only spare half an hour for questions. Luckily, after just 15 minutes, the questions came to an end. This left John an extra quarter of an hour for encouraging the great democratic debate. *31 March 1988*

○○

In which the Sketchwriter spends an election day in Belfast, enjoying a Press conference with Mr Paisley in the Morning and a Stroll with Mr Adams in the Afternoon

TOGETHER on the same platform, Ian Paisley and Jim Molyneaux resemble a grotesque music hall double act. Mr Paisley looks like a large fish, a sabre toothed cod, perhaps, and next to him Mr Molyneaux, petite, purse-lipped and with the faintest suspicion of mascara about his eyes, is the timid but determined wife from a novel by Trollope.

Mr Paisley talks like a particularly wrathful God. "We must right the great wrong that has been done to Ulster", he bellows, his voice hinting at the mixture of hurt and threat that occurs when a beast is wounded. Mr Molyneaux, on the other hand, talks like a tired machine. Even when he speaks of British Ministers who would turn their own grandmothers into soup, he does so in the tone of one learning English from an ancient text.

At yesterday's press conference, Mr Paisley brandished a letter on

Downing Street writing paper from Denis Thatcher to an acquaintance of Mr Paisley who was lumbered with the loaded name of Mrs Ireland.

"I think that it reveals the *very heart* of Maggie Thatcher", said Mr Paisley. He then read out the courteous missive, in which Mr Thatcher made the mistake of writing: "Does one hear the same cry in Northern Ireland of *our* grievous loss of officers and soldiers of our army. . ." thus intimating that Northern Ireland is another country.

Denis Thatcher's words recited by Mr Paisley had all the incongruity of a paragraph of Wodehouse recited by one of the Beastie Boys. His subsequent commentary on the letter was full of all the wrath he could muster, which is a lot.

Mr Paisley is not a man without humour, though a laugh from him is like a threat from anyone else. At the end of the conference, a mild-mannered Dutch journalist introduced himself. "Your King William caused us a lot of difficulty", Mr Paisley bellowed, "but he did a good job. Before your time, of course."

The Dutch journalist, smiling, asked Mr Paisley a question about violence. His answer could have been heard down the full stretch of a medium sized airport runway. "*Don't come from the Netherlands and read me a homily about the condemnation of violence! Your country does not recognize the ballot box! You wish to destroy the ballot box! Do your research sir!*"

In the council house that was acting as the Sinn Fein headquarters in Glencolin in west Belfast, a reproduction of Constable's "The Hay Wain" looked out on the sitting room. Outside, fierce graffiti proclaimed the Republican sympathies of the area. Gerry Adams' reinforced London taxi, plastered in Sinn Fein posters, stood waiting.

Mr Adams' spruce appearance – layered hair, neat beard, tweed cap, red tie, smart shoes – contrasted with the gnarled and nicotined faces about him. He might have been a sociology professor in a football crowd, or a novice priest among natives. He has an easy and relaxed manner, and is not above being photographed with babies, though afterwards he jokes: "He'll never get a job in the shipyard now!"

From out of the reinforced taxi, Irish music played. Smiling and joking, Mr Adams confirmed that this was where his agent had been shot a week ago.

Did Mr Adams think that Mr Paisley was an evil man? Ian Paisley was like a witch doctor exploiting people's fears, he said, and he dreaded to think how many young loyalists had ended up in prison because of him, but whether he was evil he could not say. Couldn't the same be said of him? No, he didn't think it could.

As the rain poured down, I asked him if he had ever met Mr Paisley. He smiled. They'd once set eyes on each other in the BBC. Gerry Adams was waiting for a lift, and when the doors opened, there was Paisley. Mr Paisley refused to get out, pressed the knob, and went up to the next floor. "I thought I might run up and down the stairs and keep him in there for ever" chuckled Mr Adams. But then, if that had happened, Gerry Adams would be running up and down those stairs for ever as well. *3 June 1987*

∞∞

Containing supporters and opponents of Television, Mr Eric Heffer and a piece of Spinach Quiche

THE Parliamentary All-Party Group for the Televising of the House of Commons threw a little lunchtime get-together in Westminster's Jubilee Room to open an exhibition in support of their cause.

Junketeers gobbling exotic sandwiches and sausage rolls, washed down with lashings of wine, were unnerved to find that their every bite and slurp was being filmed, by an imported camera team, for immediate transmission on screens dotted around the room. The cameras, technicians and chomping faces on the screens were there to show how very unobtrusive television could be, the assembly was informed.

"I'm sure it'll be the same success with the viewers as the House of Lords has been," said the endearing Mr Merlyn Rees, Labour MP for Leeds South and Morley, in his introductory speech. Placards on the wall proclaimed that the House of Lords is watched by "up to 500,000 people", although leading statisticians in the room calculated that the numbers one, two and three can all lie somewhere "up to 500,000".

A surprisingly small number of MPs turned up, among them a surprising number of small MPs. The exception was Mr Eric Heffer, Labour MP for Liverpool, Walton. Mr Heffer was the self-elected spokesman for those against the whole idea. "I tell you now," he grunted, after Mr Rees had politely asked if anyone wanted to say anything, "I tell you now unless there is a channel continuously transmitting the House of Commons I will never vote for it."

This shock announcement sent shudders around the few television watchers in the room. Mr Heffer in the morning, Mr Heffer in the afternoon, Mr Heffer at night. As the picture of him downing a piece of spinach quiche in a couple of mouthfuls whizzed its way around the screens, it was felt that there should be safeguards set up by the IBA to prevent the under-aged and the mentally unstable from viewing such adult material.

After one or two other members had had their say, Mr Heffer plunged in again. "Take this BBC thing in the mornings," he said.

"Talk a little louder, Eric," said a Tory MP close behind him.

He talked a little louder: "Take this BBC thing in the mornings." This was believed to be a reference to *Yesterday in Parliament*. He didn't like it

[121]

because it concentrated on the dramatic performers among the members rather than what he called "the Bill Joneses" who might speak only once a year, and who "may have made a mundane speech in one sense but may have said the most important thing in another" and who "might have spoken more sense than those of us who may be considered some sort of great sort of political figures".

After everyone else had had their say, Mr Rees made a genial summing-up. As he spoke, the following statements were among those to issue loudly from under Mr Heffer's breath: "True, absolutely true"; "Of course"; "Not quite true"; and "That's the point I was making."

An hour later, a live edition of the proposed long-running television series was paraded in the main chamber of the House of Commons, with all the principal performers on parade. Television critics pronounced this unscripted run-through desperately under-rehearsed and over-long, with few of the protagonists knowing their lines.

The scripts and plotlines were judged unpromising, the leading characters unbelievable, the themes untrue to real life and many of the supporting actors wooden and unconvincing. Nevertheless, with extensive brushing-up and a lot of recasting, something presentable might be cobbled together, although the proposed continuous broadcasting would probably be considered rather less appropriate than, say, a quarter of an hour every other week.

Newcomers to the series found the story hard to follow. Obviously the main character, Mr Dennis Skinner, Labour MP for Bolsover, is the leader of one party and Mr Nicholas Soames, Conservative MP for Crawley, is leader of the other, but who are all the others meant to be?   *4 November 1987*

<hr />

Containing supporters and opponents of Capital Punishment, with another Appearance by Mr Eric Heffer

AFTER a ten-day-break, members resumed their seats, some brown, almost all, as usual, browned off. As a reward, they had been granted a debate on Capital Punishment to ease them into the new term. It was to start at five-ish, but some of them could not wait until then. No, after ten days' purgatorial abstinence, they could not wait another minute before losing their tempers.

First, Mr Fowler lost his with Ms Short. She was "typically and absolutely wrong" about something or other. Seconds later, a Labour back-bencher lost his with those who enjoyed a cigarette while working.

It seemed likely that if everyone could get so worked up about a quiet

[122]

puff or two on the factory floor, the promise of a full debate on the Death Penalty would most certainly end in tears, probably in prosecutions, and perhaps even in the need to implement its own new rulings. Cold-hearted observers, who appreciate the purple faces and flying fists of everyday constructive debate in the Chamber, smiled keenly in anticipation. Only an hour to go.

Mr Kinnock lost his temper with Mrs Thatcher, who in turn lost hers ("he hasn't listened to what I said") with him. Mr Eric Heffer was called to speak. Mr Heffer is one of those members who seems to lose his temper even as he speaks. His questions begin with the pleasantries of one who simply wishes to pass the time of day. "All the people of this country. . ." he began, for he likes to speak for everybody, ". . .were absolutely delighted by the atmosphere in Moscow." But somehow the very act of speaking in Parliament causes Mr Heffer to grow angry, so that by the end of his sentence he is always saying something a trifle uncalled for ". . .nauseated by her attitude to. . .double standards in relation to. . ." In a way, Mr Heffer had not so much lost his temper as regained his normal composure.

"Yes, I did say 'thank you' to President Reagan – and it's a great pity he can't do the same!" screeched the Prime Minister, growing ratty. Mr Heffer glared back at her with a fresh load of contempt, each of the pearls on her necklace symbolising for him a bagful of nuclear weaponry, a company privatized, a meal snatched from the mouth of a toddler in arms.

In future, Mr Heffer could follow Mr Speaker, the Serjeant at Arms and the Chaplain on their daily procession through the Central Lobby, and, as the Serjeant ritually bears his mace, so Mr Heffer might follow, his arms akimbo, ritually bearing his grudges.

And so it went on, with everyone as angry as can be, their ten-day scouting holidays seeming to have provided no fresh fuel for their angsts. Mr Skinner was cross with "the gnomes of Zurich", Mr Cryer with "this grubby government", Mr Dalyell with ministerial deceptions and Mr Benn with everyone, everywhere. Temper! Temper! With their recent abandonment of all-in wrestling, things were looking good for the television companies. And then – tarantara! – Capital Punishment at last put its head around the door. The ghouls in the gallery took out their knitting in blissful anticipation.

Oh, dear. Suddenly, everyone seemed to beam at each other, haloes of reasonableness circling above their heads. No matter how much the ghouls wished those haloes to fall a foot or two, thus encircling a few necks, they were disappointed. The Proposer was Mr Roger Gale, who, in an earlier life, had been the Producer of BBC TV's Blue Peter, and whose annoyingly calm, Aran jersey-manner owed much to a close study of Mr John Noakes. To be served Blue Peter when a Video Nasty is promised is a most terrible thing, a crime no decent ghouls can tolerate.

Mr Gale spoke of conscience and morality and the possibility of error and "a time and a place for each Member of this House to exercise his, or her, personal judgement." Should he ever lose his seat, he might consider playing the role of St Thomas More in *A Man for All Seasons*, or, like so many of those once associated with Blue Peter, he might be suited to the selling of soap-powders, with the Ultimate Detergent taking the place of the Ultimate Deterrent.

Mr Hurd, in reply, was every bit as hopelessly reasonable, quoting statistic after statistic, arriving at "no clear conclusion" and inviting the House to do likewise. Mr Gale had earlier suggested that hanging might be a little inhumane, preferring something a little more discreet. Perhaps he and Mr Hurd might consider nipping along to the Condemned Cell and humanely boring the poor offender to death.   *8 June 1988*

In which Mr Tam Dalyell expresses no small Distaste for Mr Bernard Ingham

MR BERNARD Ingham is an odd fellow who sits slumped at the side of the Press Gallery during Prime Minister's Questions, immoderately busy. He is large and craggy and rather loopy-looking, like one of the background soldiers who used to be employed on *Dad's Army*. He takes notes with such diligence that it is as if he were sitting an O level. Afterwards, the press circle around him listening to his every word, like schoolboys touting for Mars bars from a demobbed prep school Latin master.

There is something so comical about his appearance, and so unremarkable about his location, that it is hard to get very worked up about him one way or another. Somehow, the proximity of such a colourful cove – his hair is a peculiar red, like a carrot with anaemia – to the Prime Minister is rather reassuring, just as the presence of a parrot on Mr Long John Silver's shoulder was rather reassuring: with him in tow, passers-by tend to think, nothing too devilish could occur. Or so it would seem.

But others think differently. For Mr Tam Dalyell, Mr Ingham is forever up to no good. Most calamities in public life, and quite a few in private life, find themselves attributed to Mr Ingham by Mr Dalyell. Judging by Mr Dalyell's questions in the House of Commons, Mr Ingham is here, there and everywhere. He it was who weighed down Mr Eddie Edwards's skis, he it was who whispered faulty messages just prior to the Charge of the Light Brigade, he it was who was spotted blowing hard and mighty at a secret location on the night of the October hurricane.

Mr Ingham first entered Mr Dalyell's life at around the time of the Westland saga, and ever since then he has been unable to stop thinking of him. In many ways, they are strikingly similar. Ungainly figures both, in another life they might hike around picturesque mountain scenery together, clad in shorts, rucksacks, Aertex shirts and sensible shoes, swapping train-spotting experiences and offering each other cups of Bovril brewed in the open air.

But fate has set them at odds. Everything that Mr Ingham does, and much that he fails to do, finds its way into Mr Dalyell's black book. At the weekend Mr Ingham seemed to have a harsh word or two to say about the press, whom he deemed to be inadequate to their task of toeing government lines. After a seething Sunday, Mr Dalyell screeched into the Palace of Westminster the very next day, his complaints at the ready. Luckily, Monday found ten minutes allotted to questions to the Minister for the Civil Service, so Mr Dalyell could sing his grievances in an appropriate setting.

Mr Dalyell always speaks as if he were a Victorian minister foretelling the very gravest of dooms for the assembled congregation, and when he enunciates the name of Mr Ingham it is as if he were pronouncing the most iniquitous sin of all. "Mister. . .Ber-nard. . .Ing-ham," he booms, and a shudder bolts around the quaking multitude. To the mild-mannered Minister for the Civil Service, Mr Richard Luce, he suggested that Mis-ter Bernard Ing-ham ought not to be classified as a Civil Servant. He wished to know, he said, "whether those who talk in the terms he did about the hysteria of the press ought not to be paid out of Conservative Party funds".

The mild-mannered minister suddenly learnt aggression. It was as if St Francis of Assisi had just screamed, "Pull its wings off!" Mr Luce accused Mr Dalyell of always seeking to "dredge up old issues", and he sought to offer a reason why. "He does it because he recognizes the Prime Minister has been such an outstanding success and is of very great integrity and because of that he is trying to undermine the whole position."

Judging by Mr Dalyell's expression – bafflement, exasperation, indignation and outrage all jostling on to his face at the same time – it seemed as if he disagreed with at least some of the main gist of Mr Luce's diagnosis. Unbowed, he began to rub his chin with his right hand, ready to fight another day, sure in his belief that as long as the madman Ingham walked the world, not a living soul could sleep in safety.   *10 May 1988*

Containing upsetting Scenes of Class Warfare after a sleepless Night

USUALLY, it's neither one thing nor the other. Members can't decide whether to be flippant or passionate, and they end up somewhere in between, flassionate or even passpant. But after an all-evening, all-night, all-morning, all-afternoon sitting, normal impulses to be dull seemed to have been abandoned. The funny members were funnier, the chippy members chippier, the snobby members snobbier.

Outward signs did not seem promising. On the little television screens which signal what's going on, it read: HOUSING BILL REPORT PAGE 47 AMENDMENT 88, hardly a crowd-puller. Inside the Chamber, there was litter everywhere, with old order papers strewn all over empty seats, and stubbly members forging their way through the detritus of old Hansards, envelopes, letters of resignation, unpaid solicitors' bills and so on.

The only person on the Conservative front bench was Mrs Marion Roe, dressed in a shiny yellow outfit with black polka dots, looking for all the world like Mr Gary Glitter after a particularly heavy night. The only other recognizable Conservative was Mr Nicholas Soames, plump and full of smiles, the debate having seen him through tea, high tea, supper, dinner, after-dinner noggins, breakfast, elevenses, brunch, lunch, and now tea again.

The Opposition benches looked similarly shambolic and unpromising, with fifteen or so members yawning and muttering to one another amid a sea of abandoned print. But it turned out to be wrong to jump to conclusions from a brief perusal of the setting; after all, *Steptoe and Son* is set in similarly drab and untidy conditions, and remains popular.

At around three in the afternoon, Mr Paul Boateng was speaking. "You cannot move in Docklands for the Porsches," he said. His colleague Mr Brian Sedgemore intervened to tell him about "three quarter of a million pound yachts in Docklands which never even see the sea". Mr Nicholas Soames was chuckling from an almost passionately sedentary positon. "It's nice to see a smile of recognition on his lips," said Mr Boateng. "It's not a real smile, because he'd really prefer to be at Ascot," said Mr Dennis Skinner. "For the price of a box at Ascot, you could house a family in London for a year," one-upped Mr Boateng.

On normal days, class warfare totters about in a grey suit of economic statistics, but now it was romping about in a state of glorious undress, and members on both sides seemed to be tickled pink by the sight. But just as such full-frontal nudity can be a source both of threat and of merriment, so the debate constantly lurched between anger and hilarity, with little in between.

On such occasions, MPs become admirable in their capacity to hold the conflicting passions of outrage and mirth in their heads at the same time: as they waved their order papers in anger, they also managed to laugh their heads off. Sometimes, it is as if the front half of the political pantomime horse, dutifully shedding rehearsed tears, is unaware that its back half is simultaneously performing an Irish polka.

Mr David Winnick spoke movingly of "people who sleep night after night in cardboard boxes under Charing Cross". But no speech is ever too moving for some Conservative backbencher somewhere not to interject with a heartless cackle. Were St Francis of Assisi himself to descend into the Chamber, there would most assuredly be a junior Conservative backbencher who would seize the opportunity to put in a good word for blood sports. "Could the Hon Gentleman tell us when he himself last made a visit to Charing Cross?" asked the obligatory backbencher. "Three weeks ago," replied Mr Winnick. "Never ask a question to which you don't know the answer!" shouted Mr Boateng, who is a lawyer in real life.

From fun to fury and back again in five seconds: after Mr Skinner had suggested that the Prime Minister should transfer her photo-opportunities from litter collection in St James's Park to visiting the down-and-outs in Charing Cross, Mr Rhodri Morgan (Lab, Cardiff West) made quite the best joke of this Parliament, suggesting that the Prime Minister was following President Kennedy's initiative in declaring "Ich Bin Ein Binliner".

"We're going to drag this Bill right through the next night and beyond," declared Mr Skinner, and Mr Winnick seemed to agree. "It may well be that Tuesday is going to be with us for many, many hours to come," he said. To an appreciative audience, it sounded like a very good idea indeed.

16 June 1988

10
OUTCASTS AND FAILURES

A Picture of the Powerlessness and Shame that is the Legacy awarded to the Outcasts and the Failures in our Society

In which Mr Michael Heseltine
Fails to find a Voter

"CAN I say hello to you, I'm Michael Heseltine, do you live here?" Mr Heseltine was pacing the length of Kensington High Street struggling to find someone – anyone – able to vote in the Kensington by-election. Striding due east from Safeways, men from the local party offices with microphones and portable telephones running hard to catch up with him, he would not let anyone pass.

"Can I say hello to you, I'm Michael Heseltine, do you live here?" Alas for Mr Heseltine, those who live in Kensington seem wise enough not to tackle its High Street for fear of heavy traffic, bustling crowds and looming politicians. Seeing the approaching chariot, the arm of Michael Boadicea outstretched in front, innocent passers-by would dart into the nearest shops. But others did not see him in time.

"Can I say hello to you, I'm Michael Heseltine, do you live here?" A security guard had been caught. "Ye-es" he said, visibly shaken, and the Conservatives surrounded him. A local at last! "Ooh, good" said Mr Heseltine, shaking and re-shaking the security guard's hand: "May I introduce your Conservative Candidate, Mr Dudley Fishburn?"

There was no stopping them now. Mr Fishburn thrust out his hand. "So whereabouts in Kensington do you live?" he asked. "Shepherd's Bush" replied the security guard. "Ah", said Mr Heseltine. "Ah", said Mr Fishburn. "That's just outside our area," said Mr Heseltine, "Nice to meet you".

Onwards, ever onwards, in search of a Kensington resident, the wheels of high politics span mercilessly round. Five elderly women at a bus stop found themselves unable to escape. "Can I say hello to you, I'm Michael Heseltine, are you going somewhere by bus?" Having isolated their motives with uncanny precision, Heseltine pressed on with his interrogation. "And you live here, do you?" No, they all lived at the other end of the bus route. "Oh, well, nice to meet you."

"Can I say hello to you?" Recognizing the familiar face from the television screen, two men with moustaches dived into the safety of the Arab Bank. The familiar face looked elsewhere. "Do you live here?" No, everyone lived somewhere else – Swiss Cottage ("That's a bit North"), Clapham Common ("That's a bit South"), Norway, Paris, anywhere but Kensington.

They thought the other side of the street might prove more profitable. "Dudley! Dudley! Over here, Dudley!" A Conservative helper had tracked down an elderly Kensington resident emerging from Marks and Spencer. Mr Heseltine reached her seconds before Mr Fishburn. "What about this poll tax?" asked the elderly resident. "May I introduce Dudley Fishburn, your Conservative candidate", said Mr Heseltine.

Three tourists from Korea wished to take Mr Heseltine's photograph. He

gave a thumbs-up sign to the camera, beaming heartily. He approached a woman selling flowers. "Do you live here?" "No, Chelsea." "Ah, just down the road." On to the next woman. "Can I say hello to you, I'm Michael Heseltine." "No speak English." "Ah."

Outside Pizza Inn, a Kensington-based Conservative voter was located. "Delighted we've had a chance to meet", said Mr Fishburn, but he couldn't think what to say next. They strode on. "Yes, I live here", said a Greek man outside Body Shop. Mr Heseltine shook his hand vigorously, his eyebrows quivering in the breeze. "But I do not vote", he added.   *30 June 1988*

In which Mr John Wakeham Fails to keep his Eyes open

IS MR JOHN Wakeham getting enough sleep at night? If not, he is more than making up for it during the afternoon. With the Prime Minister safely away in Hanover, he took her place at the Despatch Box, bleary-eyed and sluggish.

Looking and sounding rather like Eeyore, Mr Wakeham chose to read most of his replies in a voice of unwavering dreariness. There was little Mr Kinnock, flapping his arms, crooning statistics and generally Welshing it up, and in front of him sat Mr Wakeham looking visibly distressed at having to leave his sleeping-bag and slippers in an antechamber.

Mr Kinnock was full of beans, lending credence to the theory that he has gone slightly barmy. The thrill of finding any disaster on the front pages that did not involve himself had obviously proved too much, and he was greeting the Balance of Payments Deficit as if it were a long-lost cousin. Wohohoho! Just three months ago, the Government had predicted a £4 billion deficit – what's their prediction now? Waheyhey!

Mr Wakeham half-opened his eyes and eased himself on to his feet. Oh, dear: he had a joke prepared. Mr Wakeham is hardly Tommy Cooper, alas, and his jokes tend to leave the House in a mournful silence. "First, of all, I'm glad to see the Leader of the Opposition safely in his place," he droned, leaving a pause for laughter. Sadly, the Government Chief Whip had failed to alert his backbenchers to this impending Wakeham joke, and they consequently remained glumly silent. Mr Wakeham ploughed on.

"Blah, blah, blah, of course, current account deficit is the counterpoint of capital inflow, blah, blah, blah." Mr Wakeham was reading his reply, word for word. It is quite normal for the Prime Minister to glance at discreet cribsheets but, even when she is reading, she adds a certain lilt to her voice which suggests that she could easily get by on her own. But from his tone of voice, it seemed likely that Mr Wakeham used prepared notes to take him through the course of every day. "Good morning, darling," Mrs Wakeham greets him as he wakes, and immediately he reaches out for his notes before producing a reply: "The current morning follows on from the previous evening which itself preceded the night and is the counterpoint to the subsequent afternoon. Predictions that it is now, or will in the future be good are thus based on a sound review of inflow, blah, blah, blah."

Mr Kinnock bounced back. "If everything is doing so well," he asked, "then why are interest rates going up?" Mr Wakeham continued his prepared speech. "Blah, blah, principal weapon in monetary policy, blah, blah, downward pressure, blah, blah."

Even Mr Dave Nellist could not breathe life into Mr Wakeham. Usually, Mr Nellist acts as a sharp dose of smelling salts to even the most soporific of

Conservatives, startling them from their slumbers into flapping their arms and twizzling their heads. No matter how hard he tried, he simply could not disturb Mr Wakeham. Mr Nellist had been watching a "millionaire gangster landlord" on the television, and he thought that the Government was "giving the green light to ruthless gangsters such as this".

Mrs Thatcher would have greeted Mr Nellist like a landlady who, faced with unruly behaviour, threatens to call the police, but Mr Wakeham barely stirred from his sleep. "Blah, blah, sure no one in the House would support criminal activities, blah, blah," he burbled.

A Labour backbencher listed an inventory of complaints against the Prime Minister – abuse of her office, crisis in the NHS, unemployment, Old Uncle Tom Cobbley's role in the Westland affair, and all – and demanded that she should come to the House and "give an account of herself". Surely this would get Mr Wakeham going – but no! "I can think of better things to do with my time than answering these questions for 15 minutes," he snored, adding those dread words, "But seriously. . ." Gradually, members began to tiptoe out, anxious not to disturb the poor man.   *29 June 1988*

In which Mr Joe Ashton Fails to convince the House of the Perils of Television

MR JOE Ashton writes a column in *The Star*. It is called something along the lines of "The Voice of Common Sense" or "I'm No Idiot" or "Come Outside and Say That". He is a bluff Northerner acting the part of the bluff Northerner. Sharp-eyed readers of his column can almost detect the beer-stains on the prose. He uses words like "daft" and "so-called" and "no-nonsense".

Mr Ashton is an opponent of the televising of the House of Commons. He thinks it would trivialize, sensationalize and bring gimmicks to the House. He made this point forcefully in a speech of almost unprecedented trivia, sensationalism and gimmickry.

"TV. . .is about the rash of showbiz" he said, deploring the trivia upon which it thrived. He then mentioned *Coronation Street* and *Eastenders*. With television, he said, you would have abseiling lesbians every day of the week. This was one of the very few times abseiling lesbians had been mentioned in the Chamber.

"I've seen a bag of horse manure being thrown in this Chamber" he went on, and many psychologists present felt that this traumatic experience might have had a profound effect on his subsequent speeches. He believed that the "deferential attitude to this House would change" as the television companies concentrated on "the stunts, the gimmicks, the excitement".

Had Mr Ashton's imaginary television company been filming the full debate, it would undoubtedly have concentrated its coverage on this particular speech. He began to complain of Parliamentary nuisances. "They show off and when they go back home they are heroes" he claimed, perhaps drawing upon personal experience.

Mr Tam Dalyell rose to interrupt. He thought that television would be of value because then "people would see the way the Prime Minister evades the Question of Westland". Mr Ashton added, after throwing a bag of bluff Northern praise at Mr Dalyell: "I have to say that the public are bored stiff by Westland".

Dear, oh, dear. Mr Dalyell looked like the primmest Crufts competitor whose pedigree entrant has just been declared a two-bit mongrel. He rose again. "They may be bored with Westland, they may be bored with the Belgrano", he choked, waving his spectacles this way and that, "but they are not bored with whether the Prime Minister tells the truth or not".

With his every blunt, Northern word, Mr Ashton seemed to ostracize yet another close colleague. At one point he complained that television would force members to be in the House from ten in the morning to three o'clock the next morning. "Still easier than the pit" interjected Mr Dennis Skinner. "I'm not talking about the pit" barked back Mr Ashton. "A lot easier, and better paid", continued Mr Skinner.

For some reason or other, Mr Ashton decided that the time had come to remind members of his own newspaper column. Observers began to suspect that his speech had been sponsored by the television companies as a cruel caricature of the worst aspects of the anti-TV lobby. "My newspaper column is read by nine million people", Mr Ashton bragged, somewhat optimistically. "The people who decide whether I write a newspaper column are the readers. If the readers stopped reading it, my column wouldn't last two weeks." No-one quite knew where to look.

Further pursuing his objective of forcing would-be supporters to switch sides, he went on to criticize the television companies for focussing on Mr Heffer's walk-out at the 1985 Labour conference after Mr Kinnock's criticism of Militant.

Mr Heffer, until then a dedicated anti-TV campaigner, rose furiously to his feet. "He didn't mention Militants, he mentioned the Liverpool City Council, and that's why I walked off", he spluttered.

Trivia, bias, misinformation, indignity, gimmickry: Parliament must tread no further along this perilous path. On no account should Mr Ashton be readmitted to the Chamber, even on an experimental basis.

10 February 1988

In which Mr John Moore Fails to become the next Conservative leader

HOW ODD to feel sorry for Mr Moore. With his gold Biro and his Rolex watch, his meaningless face and his rootless voice, he is not a man upon whom sympathy alights with ease. But as he spluttered and croaked his way through the cackling of the opposition and the snoozing of many of his colleagues, it was hard not to feel a twinge of sorrow.

After Mr Robin Cook for the Opposition had nonchalantly listed an extraordinary number of diseases and ailments for which Mr Moore was to be blamed, the Secretary of State for Social Services took a swig of water and began his defence.

"Health and illness, as I know to my personal cost, arouse deep emotion", began Mr Moore. The word "emotion" came out as "em-oh-oh-tion", and for a second it seemed as if he might be the second British politician within the space of a week to burst into tears. But as his speech went on, it became clear that he was still ill: every few minutes he would take another sip of water, and every few seconds his voice would grow hoarser and hoarser.

Alas, by the end of his speech it seemed likely that his malady was not confined to the purely physical, but that his mind was entertaining the most bizarre hallucinations: to his burbling there was no end, to his sense, no beginning.

"They don't mean to hurt", he said of the party opposite. Having listed the drop in pay in real terms of ancillary staff, administrative staff, doctors, dentists and nurses under the last Labour government, he screeched: "We saw investment in the Health Service sla-a-a-ashed!"

"Is this the record of which they are prou-ou-oud?" he choked, reaching for more water.

Throughout his speech, members on all sides chatted away. At one point, a private argument between Mr Tebbit and Dr Owen, conducted grinningly across the floor of the House, seemed to attract greater attention than the main event. Labour members were popping up every few seconds asking the Minister to give way on this point or that; others merely shouted their objections while still seated.

"More water! More water!" Mr Tony Newton, to the Minister's left, demanded urgently upon seeing the decanter run dry.

Amidst all these distractions, Mr Moore seemed quite lost, like a child wandering alone at the zoo looking for his mother. Sad to say, some mothers have been known to tiptoe post-haste from the zoo to the comfort of home, where, feet up, they quite relish the possibility of young John tottering into the teeth of a tiger. Young John strayed from his speech to answer two points from the Opposition.

First, contrary to rumour, he was in full agreement with Mr Major: "There is no difference between us at all, Mr Speaker, there is no difference between us at a-a-all. Quite the reverse".

Second, the private treatment for his recent illness: "Throughout my adult life I have been able to benefit from the service. Every member of my family has used the National Health Service and continues to use it. I will never forget the staff of St Helier's Hospital where my mother died of cancer. When I choose not to burden the health service, not to force myself on it, it is regarded as wrong, and this is one of the reasons the party opposite will never again govern!"

It is strange that a man can be at turns loopy and gratuitous, self-righteous and paranoid, indignant and fist-banging, and yet still remain a cardboard figure, flimsy and featureless and, perhaps, easily disposable. His speech was full of non-statements of pseudo-consensus: "What, then, is the way forward?" and "We must see them more as opportunities rather than problems." Occasionally, it seemed as if this blank screen of a man had been programmed into a faulty system, the words going haphazard and haywire. "A serious attempt to turn out proper in fact", he said at one point, a phrase which he then tried to correct by saying: "I'm groping for one word only, which is the responsibility and the record this government ha-a-as".

Up in the public gallery, five men in white coats looked on with unusual interest.   *20 January 1988*

In which Mr John Moore Fails again, this time in Verse

WITH apologies to Charles Wolfe's "The Burial of Sir John Moore at Corunna"

Not a cheer went up, not a rejoicing note,
As his brief to the Despatch Box he carried;
Not a dry eye was there to welcome him home,
O'er a hospital bed he had tarried.

His eyebrows were raised, his hands all aquiver,
As the sods with their bayonets turning,
Glared back at him with blood in their eyes,
The revival preceding the burning.

[135]

With Edwina beside him, dressed all in yellow,
He advanced in a bit of a hurry,
And as Mr Skinner proceeded to bellow,
Moore leant back on cash, and on Currie.

"He's the potential leader!" screamed Skinner,
While Moore burbled of great health improvements,
But to judge an MP by his words is all wrong:
There is more to be told from his movements.

His face it is blank, his blue tie is neat,
A slight flush can be seen on his cheek.
But though his jaw juts and his gestures are tough
His impressions of strength comes out weak.

"The government's making this country sick"
Moaned a disgruntled Labour backbencher.
Moore twiddled his biro and looked down at his brief,
As if happy to bow to such censure.

"Increased Patient Activity" were his words of the day,
A catchphrase not destined to stick:
Quoits and basket-ball and tennis and squash
Form unwelcome demands on the sick.

Percents and percents and percents and percents;
You could only but swoon at Moore's grasp!
But even the merriest percentage of all
Will not cheer up a patient's last gasp.

And so the Prime Minister took to her place,
This century's most long-standing resident,
Her visit to Africa taking its toll
As she addressed Mr Speaker as "President".

Slowly and smoothly Moore laid himself down,
From the field of his fame fresh and gory,
But the smooth and the slippery are closely allied,
So we left him alone with his glory.

13 January 1988

In which Mr Roy Hattersley Fails to win Hearts or Minds

MR BENN is far from being the giggly type, and on the platform at the Labour Party conference this week his face has shown few signs of mirth. Were Mr Kinnock to yelp with pain having sat upon a Labour rose, Mr Benn might conceivably manage a titter, though at the same time he would not wish to risk the wrath of the pro-flowerist lobby.

So delegates were cheered to see him beam with pleasure in the early hours of the afternoon. He had much to be happy about. First, his son Hilary had taken the rostrum. Second, Hilary was continuing the family tradition of scattering the word "accountable" all over his speech with all the diligence of an Italian waiter with a pepper-pot to hand.

Though Hilary Benn has the face of a younger Sir Eldon Griffiths, his eyes are those of his father – whirling dervishes spinning on a taut grey canvas. Many of his gestures, too, are familiar, including the dice-roll of the hand and the upwardly mobile eyebrows. And like his father, his choice of necktie is restricted to those carrying the emblem of a prescribed union.

He was speaking in the education debate, and the words "freedom and liberty for all" and, more particularly, "locally accountable" seemed to bring tears to his father's eyes. But within minutes he had returned to the crowd, and Mr Benn senior, with only the prospect of Mr Roy Hattersley to see him through the day, returned to looking grim.

Mr Hattersley's speech was reminiscent of a long swim through a sea of mashed potato. He began by saying "profoundly" twice in the same sentence, once with the additional burden of his humorous irony: "We should be profoundly grateful to Mrs Thatcher". Leaning over his lectern like a walrus about to gobble, he said that "Mrs Thatcher has proved that education is a profoundly political issue". He then added that the socialist educational system offered "new choices, new prospects, new horizons and new hopes".

Observers noticed in this statement a marked change of policy: he was obviously heralding a significant increase in the number of similes the Labour party could squeeze into one sentence. Later, he was to demand that blacks in schools should be treated with "the same respect, the same value, the same worth". Experts interpreted this as a 25% retreat from his previous position.

His speech was a nightlight for the insomniac. Sympathisers remarked that he had read it through before delivering it, though others dismissed this as a rumour put about by his highly sophisticated public relations machine. Speaking with his eyes fixed to the text, every now and then he would jerk his head backwards and his eyes upward in a vain attempt to convince the audience that he was still alive.

"We can't afford the waste that is the inevitable result of selection", he was heard to say, but leading restaurateurs among the delegates believed the key word was less likely to have been "waste" than "waist", and that he was arguing for the *table d'hôte* over the *à la carte*. Around this stage, he raised his voice: "I AM IN FAVOUR OF GREATER CHOICE IN EDUCATION", perhaps to disguise an impending tummy-rumble.

". . .without inhibitions, without embarrassment, without regret". As the paragraphs became more and more packed with words whose meanings were growing more and more alike, the suspicion loomed that his speech had begun the day as no more than a single little sentence, skipping and jumping in its trite frivolity. Now, force-fed on a diet of Roget's Thesaurus, it had become a lumbering beast, unable to walk, fit only to grunt and whimper.

1 October 1987

⋙∞∞∞∞∞∞∞∞∞∞∞∞∞∞∞∞∞∞∞∞∞∞∞∞∞∞∞∞∞∞∞∞∞∞∞∞∞∞⋘

In which Mr Tam Dalyell
Fails to ask a New Question

MR TAM Dalyell sometimes sits with a picnic of papers surrounding his person. Folders and files, manila envelopes, writing papers, more folders, more files, diaries, old Hansards, newspapers and magazines are all littered around. He then sifts through them haphazardly, barely looking up as the important matters of the day are discussed by surrounding members. A Dalyell picnic can mean one of two things: either he has no interest in speaking or listening, and is merely using the green benches of the House of Commons as a suitable lawn on which to feast on his files, or else he is so anxious to speak that he has brought his feast to work so as not to miss his moment.

As Sir Geoffrey Howe meandered gently onwards through the problems of the world, Mr Dalyell was unpacking his hamper and spreading it all about. From some way above, even the most eagle-eyed observers found it hard to discern the exact magazine he had drawn from a brown envelope and was now browsing through. With its glossy paper and plentiful pictures, it might well have been a women's fashion magazine, which would account for the swiftness with which this unfrivolous gentleman returned it to its envelope. Next to be opened was a dull-looking manuscript with a small House of Commons note stapled to it. After a quick flick, Mr Dalyell returned this, too, to its envelope, folded it and placed it in the rack in front of him.

Mr Kaufman was now attacking Sir Geoffrey Howe over the Government's attitude to South Africa. Mr Dalyell had begun to place crosses against a printed list of names. Who were these names, and why was Mr

Dalyell crossing them? These were just two of the questions raised by Mr Dalyell's actions during the afternoon. We shall probably never gain a direct and conclusive answer.

Into the rack went the crossed names and out came a pamphlet entitled "Defend the NHS". He perused this carefully for about five seconds before returning it to its envelope, folding the package in half and placing it in the rack. He then brought out a large plastic file, filled top-to-bottom with a variety of manuscripts and papers. At times like these, Mr Dalyell bears an uncanny resemblance to Miss Amelia-Anne Stiggins, who, you will remember, stuffed her umbrella full of delicious sweetmeats to take back to her poor little brothers and sisters.

Mr Dalyell's poor little Liberal brother, Sir Russell Johnston, began to peer greedily across the aisle at the large duplicated sheets of typescript Mr Dalyell now held in his hands. Mr Dalyell was writing a list on House of Commons notepaper of matters arising from the duplicated typescript. Would this list form the basis of a spine-chilling question to a senior minister? It was still hard to tell whether this was to be a day of action for Dalyell or not.

As the duplicated sheets went into the rack, which had now begun to resemble an extravagant form of brown-paper Christmas decoration, Sir Geoffrey spoke of the future of Hong Kong. Meanwhile, Mr Dennis Skinner sat himself down on the aisle next to Mr Dalyell and whispered, a most unusual form of communication for the Hon Member for Bolsover. As his cocked left ear received Skinner's whispers, Mr Dalyell's eyes darted hither and thither, ever on the lookout for MI5 plants.

Mr Skinner returned to his seat. Mr Dalyell began tearing a page out of an old Hansard and placing it in yet another envelope, and Mr Jeremy Corbyn started publicly to condemn President Reagan. Mr Dalyell then put all his papers to one side, replaced his fountain pen in his pocket, and, rubbing his hands, leant forward in his seat, his traditional starting position.

At last his moment had come. He leapt to his feet. "A point of order, Mr Speaker," he intoned, "on a new question of parliamentary procedure!"

"It's not a new question at all," Mr Speaker replied, forgetting to ask what it was. And so Mr Dalyell, eyebrows raised high in indignation, returned to lists, his crosses and his torn old Hansards.   *4 February 1988*

A short sketch in which Mr Tam Dalyell Fails to get Thrown out

MR TAM Dalyell, wearing the face of a senior chicken undergoing a particularly uncalled-for strangulation, sat agitatedly through Questions to the Chancellor. He had tabled the first question to the Prime Minister on the forgotten subject of Westland. Rumour had it that he intended to be thrown out of the House due to intemperate language. Mr Dalyell's particular form of protest favours the forgotten. Were he a chef, he would produce the Christmas pudding well into March. Soon he will be asking for a full-scale public inquiry into Mrs Thatcher's role in the Suez crisis, not forgetting her disgraceful backstage shenanigans during the Tolpuddle Martyrs affair.

Mr Dalyell is by nature a fidget, but never more so than when teeing up to abuse the Prime Minister. On to the nose go the spectacles, into the ear goes the tip of the pen, off come the spectacles, and it's into the mouth with the pen. This absurd juggling act had the addition of a spectacle case, an order paper, a notepad, ten fingers and a couple of elbows. Observers noted that, with the addition of a dancing bear, he must surely stand an even chance of an executive post in a leading touring circus.

Conservative protester Mr Geoffrey Dickens rose to his feet. In a dramatic departure from his usual brief, Mr Dickens failed to mention a television soap opera, "littul cheeldrun" or any incident headlined in the tabloid press of the previous day. However, he does not gracefully pass over an opportunity to make an idiot of himself, and once again he lowered to the occasion, ever the night-club bouncer falling backwards into the fancy cake.

"Given the cleaner emissions from power stations," he emitted, uncleanly, "is it not the time to privatize fresh air?" Alas, there was no studio co-ordinator to proffer the sign saying "Laugh", so his joke was followed by an ear-shattering outburst of silence.

Observers and rumour-mongers expecting much from Mr Dalyell's confrontation with the Prime Minister came away as disappointed as ghouls after the man on the ledge has decided to nip back in for another year or two. Mr Dalyell spluttered a polite question and sat back in his place, all that shuffling and juggling gone to waste. It emerged later that Mr Kinnock, not wishing the sheen to be taken off his own questions to the Prime Minister, had urged propriety upon poor Mr Dalyell. *30 October 1987*

In which Mr Robert Maclennan
Fails to convince the House of his Charisma

POOR Bob. There are those people in the world for whom the word "poor" becomes less a description than a supernumerary Christian name. Finding themselves prefixed with "poor" is made all the more humiliating for having been born of some sort of jocular sympathy. Poor Bob Maclennan has joined their number.

Poor Bob's first shock of the day must have been to find Mr Ken Livingstone as his new next-door neighbour. Mr Livingstone usually skulks, sheafs of correspondence in hand, in a lonely position somewhere around the middle of the Labour benches. He has now joined the punks on the alternative front bench, setting up home with Skinner, Sedgemore and Cryer. At the end of that bench, neat and well-manicured, sits Poor Bob. So now he has to suffer Mr Livingstone, as young Albert once had to suffer the Lion.

As the Secretary of State for Defence went about defending the Prime Minister ("I would have thought that the Hon Member would find congratulations in order on today of all days. . ."), Poor Bob was handed a large envelope by a messenger. Well-wishers were hoping that it would prove to contain something seasonal and reassuring such as an advent calendar or a bit of tinsel; alas, it looked long and printed and unhappy – possibly a draft merger agreement. Poor Bob.

Reading through this momentous agreement, Mr Maclennan must have been distracted by the irreverent chuckles of Sedgemore and Skinner. Only the entrance of Mrs Thatcher can have allowed his mind to concentrate on higher things.

Mr Heseltine loomed to his feet, Tarzan in retirement, reduced to scurrying about collecting other gents' mugs and wishing them all the very best as they beetle off to more important business. "Would the Hon Lady accept the congratulations from this side of the House for. . ."

"He's only after a job" butted in Mr Skinner, always so *unnecessary*.

After a Labour backbencher had described the Prime Minister as "President Reagan's tea-lady", Poor Bob rose to his feet, his right hand in his jacket pocket with thumb poking out, a pose intended to suggest the look of a statesman, but erring rather more closely towards the look of a secret hitchhiker.

"Oooooh!" went those MPs who can be described as bullies, all six hundred of them, "OOOOOOOOH!!!" His head jutting upwards in stationary dignity, Poor Bob began his important speech. It sounded like this: ". . . . ." and continued like this: ". . .. .", drowned out, as it was, by that incessant "OOOOOOOOH!"

The Speaker of the House, a kindly man, attempted to come to Poor

Bob's rescue. "Order! Order!" he said, adding, "The Hon Member *is* leader of his party".

In all great tragedies, it is the acts of unselfish kindness by bystanders which produce the greatest tears. And the greatest hoots of laughter too. Had Mr Speaker reminded the House that the Hon Member *was* a fried egg or that the Hon Member *was* a Mexican jumping-bean, he could not have provoked more riotous guffaws. "WAHAHAWAHAWAHAHAW-WAHAHA" went the House. Onlookers, who pressed their ears to their personal amplifiers could just make out the following words from Poor Bob: ". . .Nuclear. . .whether she will. . .talks. . ."

Ever gracious, the Prime Minister pretended to have heard Poor Bob's wise thoughts. "Absolutely vital", she agreed. Poor Bob, now seated, nodded statesmanlike agreement, his hand clutching firmly at his knee.

Later, as the House began gradually to empty, Mr David Steel walked out past Poor Bob. Poor Bob attempted to catch his eye, but Mr Steel seemed to have other things on his mind. While Mrs Thatcher spoke of grain surpluses, Poor Bob placed his hand over his mouth and then looked up towards the Press Gallery. Perhaps he would find some comfort there. But no: they were just as likely to snigger too. Poor Bob.   *9 December 1988*

In which Mr John Major Fails to keep the House on the edge of its Seat

IT WAS a day like any other, but it seemed to last several weeks. Jeremy Corbyn (Lab, Islington North) wasn't wearing a jacket or tie, a state of undress that once again unduly upset Mr Anthony Marlow (Con, Northampton North).

Mr Tam Dalyell was perplexed about the amount of blowpipes in Afghanistan. Mr Andrew MacKay (Con, Berkshire East), who bears some resemblance to the type of fresh-faced god-fearing youth so often found with the gun in his hands after a presidential assassination, asked Opposition members to "stop whingeing".

The bearded Mr Martin Flannery (Lab, Sheffield, Hillsborough) complained that he was only getting "small tinkles" from his British Telecom telephone, and was it not a disgrace? Miss Clare Short (Lab, Ladywood) said that there was no reason for the House to imitate a boy's public school and that dress regulations were ridiculous.

These are all events that seem to happen every day, like the coming up of the sun and the going down of the moon. But one doesn't hear a speech from Mr John Major, Chief Secretary at the Treasury, on finance every day. Were such a prospect to be included in the Commons procedure on a regular basis, the sun might well decide not to come up, and the moon would simply switch itself off.

Mr Major is grey and tall, but mainly grey. His prose style suggests that he has yet to read the works of Ronald Firbank; his delivery is that of a doctor with indifferent news for a patient for whom he has no particular feelings.

By the end of his Opening Speech for the Second Reading of the Finance Bill, the sparse chamber was so thoroughly somnolent that the massed bands of the Coldstream Guards could have heralded the entry of the entire cast of "Ben Hur" and not even the most energetic member would have managed to bat an eyelid.

"Essentially, however, these proposals are the same and they represent a significant initiative. They form an important and imaginative element in our strategy to improve the supply performance of the economy. . ."

This came towards the beginning of Mr Major's speech, when the world still seemed fresh and bright-eyed. By the end, the chamber looked as if an alien force had preyed hideously upon all members: the lucky ones had disappeared entirely, and the few who remained, their faces horribly swollen, their bodies immobile, were mute and dispossessed.

"There is no quick and easy solution. . ." At this, Mr John Wakeham, the new Leader of the House, appeared to slump forward, while the Chancellor of the Exchequer began chatting to a backbencher behind him.

It might have been the Annual Summer Ball of the Tired Phrases. Other members were opening buff envelopes, sauntering through *A La Recherche du Temps Perdu*, planning and creating a family, or whatever they could fit in during the time available.

"Finally", Mr Major said, and triumphant cherubims seemed to fly through the upper windows trumpeting messages of goodwill to all men on earth, "there are a few fairly minor changes to the Bill which I should mention briefly".

At this point, Mr Nicholas Soames (Con, Crawley) came in, a big bundle of envelopes under his arm, hardly a cherubim, but nonetheless a welcome diversion. ". . .There are also a couple of amendments to the Finance Act passed before the election. . ." Mr Major continued, and Mr Soames's left shoe began to slip from his left foot, revealing a bright yellow sock.

"A measure of counter arrangements to circumvent. . ." Mr Major said. Would the shoe fall or would Mr Soames notice in time? Sometimes these apparently trivial details assume a position of such importance that they command the whole of one's attention.   *9 July 1987*

A short Sketch, in which Mr Edward Heath hovers Alone around the Conservative Conference

THE delegates' eyes flickered with recognition as the phantom footsteps came close and closer still. The shoulders – *those shoulders* – heaved and heaved again, the mouth let loose the terrifying grin. Around the phantom swirled burly security guards in their City gent suits, the disguise flawed only in the flairs.

He's here – here among us! That death-defying laugh, livid in its intensity. That hair, spooky in its strange whiteness. And then, final confirmation, that voice, a cat whining its death knell.

"Funny thing, I thought I saw an ex-Prime Minister today", Young Conservatives would tell their ashen-faced parents. "Nonsense, darling – he never existed and you must never, never tell such awful stories again", their parents would reply.

Yet there he was. The Right Honourable Mr Edward Heath, in broad daylight, strolling confidently through the corridors of the conference hall, his hand outstretched in a gesture of camaraderie as old colleagues darted into the shadows.

And all who heard should see them there,
And all should cry, "Beware! Beware!
His flashing eyes, his floating hair!"

As he hovered past the stalls, onlookers could but guess at his stopping-off points. To his left was a Conservative souvenir stall. Nothing to take exception to there, one might have thought: Conservative Egg Cosy (£1.75), Conservative Oven Glove (£3.95), Conservative Lavender Sachet (99p), Blue Rosette Casual Wear Jogging Suit (£29.95). The traditional Christmas Greetings card depicting a one-parent underprivileged ethnic family in an inner city deprived housing situation might have seemed needlessly Moaning Minnie, but it was properly counterbalanced by a pleasant view of Buckingham Palace in the evening sun.

But Mr Heath hovered onwards, casting little more than a glance in the stall's direction. "I Love Maggie", ran the slogan on a T-shirt. "I Love Maggie", ran the slogan on a mug.   *7 October 1987*

In which Mr Edward Heath appears once more, this time as a Beverley Sister

WITH his bright silver hair contrasting peculiarly with his bronzed face, Mr Edward Heath (Con, Old Bexley and Sidcup) resembles a Beverley Sister gone to seed as he listens to young Tory after young Tory fawn and squelch to Mrs Thatcher.

He sits motionless in his slip-on shoes, right finger pressed to forehead, hand obscuring face, his eyes never quite closed, never quite open, the whole a curious mixture of sadness and self-sufficiency. When members on one side or another are hooting with laughter or shaking with anger, Mr Edward Heath never smiles. But nor does he show disapproval. He simply stares straight ahead, an island inaccessible to others. As Mrs Margaret Thatcher speaks, he stares straight ahead, as if wishing to avert his eyes while this temporary fault is adjusted. Even when she blunders and the Opposition howl, he remains impassive, giving nothing away. At inter-party jokes, free from the taint of political bias ("Has the Prime Minister found time to read the Saturday edition of the Leicester Mercury?"), he looks down at his order-paper, the headmaster turning a blind eye to such tomfoolery.

Next to him, the fading stars of Thatcherism make merry. Mr Heseltine whispers to Mr Tebbit, and then both roar with naughty laughter. Behind him, even Mr Leon Brittan (erroneously described by the Speaker as "Mr Loin Brittan") quite regularly smiles. But Mr Heath prefers to listen intently (or is he listening? who can tell?) to Mr Jeremy Corbyn glumly rattling on about hypothermia rather than associate himself with the frivolities of the powerless.

As the Education Reform debate was launched, his hand was rather more active than usual, jotting things down on loose sheets of paper, though his face remained devoid of any expression beyond a kind of lonely superiority.

At the Despatch Box, Mr Kenneth Baker smarmed and enunciated his way through a long, written speech in praise of his own particular brands of choice, quality, freedom and standards. Occasionally, Mr Heath's head would turn leftwards towards him, the corners of his eyes bestowing upon the Secretary of State for Education a look of something approaching, or even surpassing, contempt. But these glances were infrequently stolen, as if the very act of their bestowal was more than the Secretary deserved. Only at one point, when Mr Baker stated "the opinion polls also clearly show its popularity" did Mr Heath afford himself an unplanned movement. His left eyebrow rose above the solemn waxiness of the rest of his face.

As Mr Jack Straw for the Opposition read his lengthy litany of off-the-peg criticism ("setting child against child, parent against parent, school against school, race against race. . .") Mr Heath sat steady and still. Eventually, Mr Straw's speech came to an end and Mr Heath loomed slowly to his feet. Though the feet remained firmly pointed to the front, his body was more often stretching backwards, for it was his own side whom he wished to chastise.

Like a history lesson delivered by a senior teacher who has never quite learnt to silence the nuisances, his speech was a compelling mixture of the high ("the great tradition of Disraeli, Balfour and Butler") and the low ("there is no point in the Member chanting like that and then grinning"). Gloom and conspiracy linked most of his sentiments ("My Rt Hon Friend shakes his head, but he knows full well the reason academics haven't spoken out is that they're afraid they'll lose their jobs"). Though his bile was reserved mainly for his allies, it was by no means exclusive to them. When Mr Neil Kinnock was seen to titter, Mr Heath rounded on him. "There is no point in the Leader of the Opposition laughing like this. . .his predecessor would have been ashamed of himself. . ."

Convinced that the limited time allowed for debate was a "caricature of parliamentary government", Mr Heath refused to give way to interventions. "There's no time, there's no time" he kept stressing. He addressed his most damning remarks towards Mr Baker in person. "I believe that this is very largely a confidence trick", he said, staring straight at the man he had been ignoring all day.

Mr Baker never exchanged his glance, preferring to sit back and let a patient smirk say it all. After all, this strange, sincere, awkward, figure, busily making the Opposition so happy and his own side so uncomfortable, could no longer change anything. And Mr Baker could.   *2 December 1987*

In which Mr Ian Paisley becomes a Grandmother

AS THE rest of the House listened to questions on choice in education, Mr Ian Paisley (Unionist, Antrim North) squashed into the corner of the Government benches and shuffled a multitude of papers, occasionally reaching for his pen and scribbling with solemn fury.

The more he scribbled, the redder his face grew, as if it were some pressure gauge for his thoughts. This red contrasted strangely with his summery light grey suit, his silvery tie, his white socks, and his white, white shoes. It was as if the Great Gatsby's wardrobe had been raided by the Big Bad Wolf, or as if Mr Hardy Amies had hastily costumed a raddled Billy Bunter.

He kept writing through every distraction – here a shoe falling from the Stranger's Gallery on Miss Clare Short, there a fit of giggles erupting

between Mr David Steel and Mr Paddy Ashdown — until questions to the Education Minister gave way to Questions to the Prime Minister.

When a Unionist asked her whether she would find time today to reflect on the Anglo-Irish Agreement (an almost daily question) it looked as if he was making to rise. But Mrs Thatcher carried on her steady path — British Telecom improving every minute, schoolchildren have their rights too — without the Reverend Big Bad Wolf ever once leaping from behind his tree.

Though it is by no means an infrequent occurrence, it always comes as a surprise to see Mr Paisley laughing. Somehow it is as incongruous as a bull tiptoeing or a snake stamping. But laugh Mr Paisley did, his face growing ever redder, as Mrs Ann Winterton (Congleton) whispered into his ear. As he laughed, he added a succession of one-liners to the lady's original joke, and she burst out laughing too. What can he have been saying to her? Perhaps he was reassuring her that he was, indeed, her grandmother.

By the end of this repartee, Mr Paisley's arm had stolen around the back of the bench, and was now placed just behind her back.

Then the Northern Ireland Orders were announced, and three-quarters of the House exited, as is their wont. Mr Tom King, Secretary of State for Northern Ireland, began a conciliatory speech full of the words "helpful", "listen" and "commitment" and the phrases "the interests of all the people", "convenient to all concerned" and "overwhelming majority".

For a time it seemed as if Mr Paisley, his body now sprawled out, his belly now pushing mightily at the thin fabric of his shirt, might remain silent. He had been joined by the spindly, dark, oddly characterless figure of Mr Peter Robinson (Belfast North), the spooky dummy sitting motionless beside the ventriloquist who once controlled him.

Mr Peter Archer, the Opposition Spokesman on Northern Ireland, repeated all Mr King's favourite words and phrases, and Mr Paisley spent his time smoothing down his hair and pulling up the zip on his trousers. And then he lumbered to his feet and spoke, his voice now croaking, now whispering, now booming, and always carrying in its undertow the potential for wrath.

He spoke of the iniquity of pubs opening on Sunday, of the freedom to fly the flag, of tombstones and poison and prejudice (the final syllable of which he rhymes with "mice"). His fist beat the air, his arms waved about, and his whispers became shouts as he spoke of the difficult road to conciliation. "If this House thinks they're going to change traditions, they cannot do it and they will not do it, and the flag will fly!" he roared.

But most of the House could not hear: they were away, possibly drinking, thinking of other things. *3 July 1988*

Containing chilling Observations on the Four Faces of Dr Owen

DR DAVID Owen has four postures while in the Chamber of the House of Commons. The most usual has him as a sun-worshipper, his legs outstretched, his bronzed head beneath the back of the bench, his arms crossed languidly. All that is missing is the Jamaica Rum Punch, the sun oil and the Shirley Conran. The second is the Skinner-like posture: hunched forward, active, ready to speak, man of the moment.

Then there is the third, and most sinister, Owen: screwed up into the side of the bench, his body circling round on itself, his hand playing conspiratorially around his chin, his face creased up, moody, vengeful, like something one might find brushing against one's face in the labyrinthine darkness of an amateurish Ghost Train. Finally, the Owen as he likes to be – The Orator, standing erect and impressive, his jacket buttoned, his head steady, his trousers beautifully pressed, his words emerging forcefully without hesitation, repetition or deviation.

Now that he is more likely to be chatting to a member of the Raucous Left than to a neighbouring Liberal, his new isolation makes the speedy movement from one posture to another more evident. During Points of Order, he could be viewed in all four positions. The matter of the moment was the publication in *The Sunday Times* of Mr Peter Wright's book, *Spycatcher*. Would Dr Owen get a chance to emit his seven favourite words – "Indeed, when I myself was Foreign Secretary"? The House was on tenterhooks.

When talk turns to conspiracies, Mr Tam Dalyell is sure to rise from his seat and point a finger of suspicion at a combination of MI5, Mrs Thatcher, the CIA, the BBC, The Joker, The Penguin and the Mayor of Gotham City. But Tam was not there! Was he even now sitting in the Outback wearing a bush hat, penning memoirs that would bring down the Government or at any rate a government?

In his place came Mr Dale Campbell-Savours, a sort of English Miss Jean Brodie. He told the Speaker that he was fearful of the obstruction of his right as an MP "to table questions which the public want to know answers to". In fact, it is one of the oddities of current affairs that the public seems less interested in knowing the answers to whether a democratically-elected British Government was conspired against by its supposed protectors than whether Miss Anne Diamond of TV-am has given birth to a boy or a girl.

Mr Tony Benn, ashen-faced and solemn, declared that he was "only anxious not to make a fool of Parliament", a rare worry for any MP. Mr Merlyn Rees asked whether Mr Wright's *Spycatcher* would be obtainable from the Library of the House. "It will be a matter for the Librarian," replied the Speaker.

And then up rose Dr Owen, spruce, dapper, buttoned. He didn't mention his time as Foreign Secretary, nor his time as Leader of a Political Party, but instead asked how any debate could take place if members were unable to read the book in question. Mr Andrew Faulds announced that he was going to order the book from the Library and exited.

A few minutes later, he returned with the news that the Librarian had been told that it was inadvisable to stock the book, but that he had put his name down for it. "If he's first in the queue, I'll certainly be second," commented The Speaker. On this basis, if the book is taken out for two weeks at a time by each member, it will be a year before the whole Cabinet has read the book, and another 26 years before all other members have read it. And by that time, Dr Owen might well be Foreign Secretary again.

14 July 1988

<hr>

In which Mr Tam Dalyell is asked to Leave, taking his Eyebrows with him

HOW AWFUL it would be to discover that one or other of the eyebrows belonging to Mr Tam Dalyell was possessed of a fear of heights. Mr Dalyell himself is a preternaturally tall gentleman, and he is always raising his eyebrows to their fullest extent. Thus, from a scared eyebrow's point of view, to be allotted to Mr Dalyell would be a terrible thing indeed.

Perhaps, in moments of relaxation beside the seaside, Mr Dalyell lowers his eyebrows. But it is hard to think of Mr Dalyell stretched out on a lilo. If perchance it sank, he would feel obliged to call for a full inquiry. If, on the other hand, it remained afloat, he would remain most uneasy. No: it is most probable that Mr Dalyell's eyebrows have been perpetually raised since first they sprouted.

Yesterday they were, to all intents and purposes, floating somewhere above his head. At first, this seemed hard to fathom, as Mr Richard Luce, in his role as Minister for the Arts, was banging on about business sponsorship, hardly the most upsetting of subjects.

But Mr Dalyell had something up his sleeve. Of course, Mr Dalyell's awkward manner of sitting – legs crossed, arms crossed, feet crossed, sometimes even eyes crossed – usually suggests he has something, perhaps an earwig or even a beehive, up his sleeve. Yesterday, however, his sleeve seemed more occupied than ever. Yes, once more that pesky fleet of Westland helicopters had settled there, and they were buzz-buzz-buzzing away.

The minute Mr Luce switched hats from Arts to Civil Service, Mr Dalyell

rose and rose and rose to his feet, eyebrows a-quiver. ". . .would it not be better for our country. . .if the Minister finally admitted that it was the Prime Minister who caused much of this trouble by telling an indispensible lie to the House of Commons."

Ooooh! There is nothing like the word "lie" to perk the Chamber up. Certainly, in an open contest between the words "lie" and "business sponsorship of the arts", "lie" wins hands down. Conservative members looked aghast. Of all the ways of looking available to Conservative members, there is none they enjoy more than looking aghast. "I ask him please to withdraw those allegations about the Prime Minister", said the Speaker. But Mr Dalyell would not.

"I believe that there is cynical corruption involved", replied Mr Dalyell. By now, observant visitors to the Strangers' Gallery could spot Mr Dalyell's eyebrows floating in the air alongside them. Below, Conservative members were yodelling their full aghastliness. "Order! Order!" went the Speaker, "I am asking him to withdraw those words".

Mr Dalyell's plummy voice boomed out. "The words were extremely carefully chosen." The Speaker gave him one last chance to withdraw the words. Then the Speaker gave him *one more* last chance to withdraw the words. "You've already given him a last chance!" shrilled Dame Elaine Kellett-Bowman, whose higher notes could smash a sheet of reinforced concrete at 20 paces. "'e's only speaking the truth!" blasted Mr Dennis Skinner, in baritone.

"I don't want to embarrass you, Mr Speaker," said Mr Dalyell, the most deeply courteous hooligan of them all, "I don't want a final chance. I wouldn't have said those words if I didn't mean them."

By this time, even sleepy old Mr John Wakeham had woken up, just in time to submit the question of Mr Dalyell's suspension to the House. While fellow members withdrew to vote on his suspension, Mr Dalyell looked grimly up towards the Press Gallery, his eyebrows now stationed somewhere just above Big Ben.

Ayes – 180! The darts score went against Mr Dalyell, whose supportive No votes scored only 28. "May I raise a point of order?" asked Mr Dalyell. "NOOOOO!" screamed the Conservatives. "Am I at liberty to – ' "NOOOO!" they screamed again. For not taking NOOOO! for an answer, Mr Dalyell was suspended and strode purposefully away. If any passing pilot discovers his eyebrows, he would be most grateful for their return.

26 July 1988

In which Mr Ken Livingstone
Names Names but No-one Notices

MR KEN Livingstone was leaning forward in his seat, tapping his fingers on the bench in front of him. That he was in his seat at all was odd enough, for it was only a week or two ago that he announced he was henceforward going to be working elsewhere. His face strangely red – the most likely origin of his "Red Ken" nickname – he looked tense and fidgety.

He is not one to ask just any old question. Not for him the complaint about cellular telephones or worries about the price of fruit. His questions tend to be rather more specific, concerning Northern Ireland and the naming of names. Once upon a time, these questions would send Tory backbenchers into contortions of fury; retractions would be demanded and often refused, tantrums would occur, headlines would be made, and Mr Livingstone would become ever more infamous.

But the naming of names by Mr Livingstone has now become rather routine. Soon he will have run out of members of the security services to name, and he will be driven to name traffic wardens, police canteen waiters and British Rail ticket inspectors. "I have it on good information that some time during the month of May he personally authorized the punching of no fewer than 700 tickets," he will reveal, before stalking out of the chamber, moustachioed, red-faced and smirkingly conspiratorial.

Alas, the chamber of the House of Commons represents a poor auditorium for a solo performer such as Mr Livingstone, for he has to wait for others to drone on before the spotlight falls on him. From Mr Livingstone's point of view, it is rather as if Hamlet, Prince of Denmark, was forced to hang about while Humpty Dumpty had his say.

The first Humpty to arise yesterday was a Conservative backbencher, furious at the "steady diet of pornography and near-pornography fed to children on a nightly basis". At times, it seems as if there must be a special satellite television station, available only to the offspring of Conservative MPs, whereon sprightly sex romps are shown morning, noon and night. Everyone else has television sets which show only a steady diet of Conservative MPs complaining about the state of television.

Mr Livingstone's fingers tapped away. Mr Harry Greenway was up again. Mr Greenway tends to speak on behalf of all those people who write furious letters to local newspapers. Not a day goes by without a fresh irritation fulminating. At least he need no longer conclude his offerings with ". . .and I will of course be informing my MP of the matter in question", for – how he must pinch himself! – he is his own MP. Handed a rose, he would declare that law-abiding citizens could sense, in its effeminate odour, the propagation of homosexuality, in its gaudy, leftish colour, a general deterioration of standards, and, in its stalk, a potentially lethal weapon of the type often employed in anti-police demonstrations.

Yesterday, Mr Greenway was upset about the shortage of parking spaces in London and worried about the effect of this shortage on, yes, "law-abiding citizens". Dear, oh dear: having to sit through all this when there were names to be named! Mr Livingstone did not look happy, and he seemed even less happy when the little Welshman on the front bench started hogging all the questions to the Prime Minister.

Mr Livingstone rose, but instead Mr Mark Fisher, Old Etonian Labour arts spokesman, was called. He spoke movingly of the plight of a 51-year-old man on a million pounds a year who paid no income tax whatsoever. This drew tears from even the most flint-hearted of Tory backbenchers. But once again, the Prime Minister would not budge.

Eventually, Mr Livingstone was called. He spoke of murder and destruction. He rammed home some unbearable truths. He named a name and, having named the name, named another name. But nothing happened: no fury, no abuse, no demands for retraction. Mr Robert Maclennan rose to speak. The rest of the House leaned forward. Aha! Something of interest at last. *20 May 1988*

In which Mr Ron Brown sits by himself

MR RON Brown was back in place, still looking rather out of place. Always something of a solitary figure – if his propensity for showering were not so well attested,* the suspicion of malodorousness might arise – he was sitting by himself, in the middle of a middle bench, busily writing notes.

Even during those periods when he is allowed into the Chamber, he is not a frequent visitor to Questions to the Minister of Agriculture, Fisheries and Food. Those tend to be somewhat sparsely populated, mainly by rural and little-known members. It is hard to cause a row or even get a little upset when the subject is sheep.

One of the advantages of Agricultural Questions is that no one else has much to say. Consequently, it is pretty easy to catch the Speaker's eye. After popping to his feet a number of times, Mr Ron Brown was eventually called. "Mr Ron BROWN!" A glimmer of interest flickered through the drowsy House as all eyes slowly turned in his direction. One or two Tory MPs even managed a cheer of sorts. It used to be that the ironic cheer was reserved solely for Mr Robert Maclennan, but now it has extended to a whole range of odd-bods: Paddy Ashdown, Alan Beith, Roy Hattersley, and now, it seems, Ron Brown.

Mr Brown speaks in a quiet, intermittently decipherable Scottish accent. "The EEC is a cynical. . .erumpherumph. . .makes people suffer. . .face facts. . .erumpherumph. . .stop kidding people the EEC matters. . .erumpherumph. . .only matters for people in big business." He speaks in a manner which suggests he is really just leading up to asking the House if it can see its way clear to lending him the cost of a cup of tea, and that his soft-spoken prefacing remarks are merely part of this larger ploy.

His short speech over, Mr Brown resumed his seat, scribbling once again on his large yellow pad. Meanwhile, Mr Harry Greenway, another urban member, called for the classification of the horse as an agricultural animal. "What animal could be more agricultural than a horse?" he asked. "A cow" came the reply from one of his fellow backbenchers. Mr Greenway ploughed on regardless.

Back to Mr Brown. All the way through Questions to the Prime Minister, he was up and down, up and down, determined to ask another question, but always others were called. Even the squashy verbosity of Mr Roy Hattersley's lolloping questions could do nothing to relax him.

Conservatives praised South Africa, the Welsh wailed about Welsh, Socialists moaned about Gibraltar, but still Mr Brown would not be diverted. Mr Eric Heffer, seeking to exit, brushed past him. Mr Heffer has a soft spot in his heart for minorities, and no minority comes smaller than Mr Brown, so Mr Heffer couldn't resist a supportive word. Beside Mr Brown, Mr Heffer appears as the archetypal capitalist, and his red braces and blue and white striped shirt lend further the impression that he may well be Mr Michael Douglas after a heavy weight has fallen on his head. Mr Brown accepted Mr Heffer's encouragement with a cheery grin.

"Mr Ron. . .Davies!" boomed the Speaker during Points of Order. Nearly, but not quite. "Mr John BROWN!" he boomed five minutes later. A Ron, and a Brown, but still no Ron Brown. It all seemed part of a cruel conspiracy, the Revenge of the Mace-Lovers. On the bench in front, Mr Dave Nellist was leaping to his feet, and, in front of him, Mr Robert Maclennan. Mr Nellist was given his turn, and, as he spoke of an aircraft crash in his constituency, Mr Brown rolled up his order paper in *angst*.

But then – "Mr RON Brown!" His persistence had been rewarded, and, perhaps in celebration, Mr Brown spoke with unprecedented clarity. "The Prime Minister has condemned trial by the media," he said. "Is it not time we had a special debate concerning the role of the press barons and the way they repeatedly pump out dishonest stories about public figures, including Hon Members of this House?" And with that he made his exit, again the solitary figure. Behind him, the others jabbered on, yet another shower he would prefer to avoid.   *10 June 1988*

---

* Fellow members had claimed to have spied Mr Brown frolicking with a lady friend in the House of Commons showers

∞∞

In which Mr Denzil Davies does not appear

"WHERE'S Denzil?" It could be the title of a popular farce, and, in a funny sort of way, it is. Running hard on the heels of that other mystery romp, "Who's Denzil?", it makes for a light-hearted sequel of enormous potential.

After a long, cold winter of dark, brooding mysteries from the Conservatives, featuring the forbidding Highsmithian anti-hero The Temperamental Mr Ridley, it seems particularly public-spirited of the Labour Party to stage a summer season of trouser-dropping, identity-mistaking, fun-loving knockabout comedies. The first of the season, "Worzel Gummidge Was My Father", seems set to lose its star and impresario Mr Michael Meacher a small fortune, but "Where's Denzil?" could well make Mr Denzil Davies a name to conjure with. That is to say, if all goes according to plan it will make him disappear.

If memory serves, Mr Denzil Davies was the Opposition spokesman on Defence, one of the very few Denzils in the history of the British Labour movement to have occupied that position. In the past month or two, he had rather slipped out of the political consciousness of the nation, so that to the vast majority of electors he was probably better known as Mr Defence

Davies, Opposition spokesman on Denzil. Nevertheless, on his occasional visits to the Chamber, he seemed a genial sort, and it surprised many that he tendered his resignation to the Press Association at one o'clock yesterday morning, explaining that he was "fed up" with Mr Kinnock who had "humiliated" him.

Where would the House be if everyone who was "fed up" with Mr Kinnock decided to throw in the towel? Certainly, the Conservative benches have shown admirable restraint in sticking it out, and Mrs Thatcher, whose irritation with the Opposition Leader grows daily more visible, still manages to face him for a full quarter of an hour, two days a week. When Mr Kinnock stood up for yesterday's confrontation, the Conservative benches seemed to join with one voice in a rendition of the title song of their new hit show:

"Where's Denzil?"

"Where's Denzil?"

"Where's Denzil?"

As show-stopping lyrics go, these seemed a mite repetitive, but at least they had everyone singing along. Mr Kinnock chose to act as if he had not yet seen the show, and could make neither head nor tail of the lyric. Perhaps secretly buoyed by the morning's tribute to his powers of humiliation, he attacked Mrs Thatcher with all the furious indignation of a Sir Harry Secombe or a Max Boyce, declaring that her attitude "manifests the mentality of a persecutor".

Oooh! For Conservative backbenchers, there was only one answer to this hurtful slight on their Leader. "Where's Denzil?" they cackled once more, now hooting with laughter. It is a sign of their deep Conservatism that they only grow to love a joke once it has been around for too long. This one will run and run until it is quite out of puff. Sir Anthony Grant, a Tory of the old school, who looks and sounds mightily like the Major in *Fawlty Towers*, had a new variation on the joke up his sleeve, and spent the first few minutes of Question Time leaping up and down in an attempt to catch the Speaker's eye. Eventually, he caught it, and out came the joke.

"Will the Prime Minister reassure the House that her relations with her Secretary of State for Defence are wholly harmonious and that he will not feel humiliated and therefore the Press Association can retire to bed at a reasonable hour?"

How they laughed! They were rolling in the aisles on all sides of the House, and even Mr Kinnock emitted one of his red-faced chuckles, giggling away like a baby with a new rattle. To his right, Mr Roy Hattersley issued one of his more sophisticated, broad-minded, man-of-the-world, yes-I've-written-a-tome-or-two-in-my-time smiles, while Mr Frank Dobson got going with his full-blooded impersonation of The Laughing Policeman.

In a desperate bid to prolong the festivities, a Labour backbencher shouted out another joke, this time even older. "Heseltine!" he yelled. Alas, the Tories didn't seem to find it very funny. Oh, dear. These things always end in tears.

15 June 1988

Index

G

Gale, Roger, 123
Gilbert, W.S., and Sullivan, A., 51
Glenarthur, Lord, 95
Glitter, Gary, SEE Roe, Marion
Gordon, Noele, 18, 81
Gorman, Teresa, 66
Gould, Brian, uncanny similarity to Mr David Jacobs, 15
Gow, Ian, 12, 80
Grant, Sir Anthony, 157
Greave, Tony, 56, 106
Greenway, Harry, as Sir Walter Raleigh, 75; as James Boswell, 82–83; as law-abiding citizen, 154; on horse, 155
Griffiths, Mrs Catherine, 37
Griffiths, Sir Eldon, 137

H

Hailsham, Lord, smirks, 98
Hall, Stuart, 32
Hamlet, Prince of Denmark, SEE Livingstone, Ken
Hammond, Eric, 60
Hanley, Jeremy, 73
Hattersley, Roy, eats bacon and tomato roll, 18–19; eats bandaged finger, 37; opens mouth, 76; and guts, 101; and lower lip, 118; and mashed potato, 137–138; 155, 157
Haughey, Charles, 85
Healey, Denis, 29–30, 61
Heath, Edward, disgruntled, 46; outcast, 144; as Beverley Sister, 145–146
Heffer, Eric, couture, 12; grunts, 37; lives in fool's paradise, 45; complains, 77; learns Welsh, 82–83; eats quiche, 121; bears grudge, 123; exits, 155
Henry the Dog, 32
Heseltine, Michael, 129–130, 141, 145, 157
Hewitt, Patricia, 61–62
Hitler, Adolf, 19
Holloway, Stanley, 51
Holme, Richard, 55, 56
Holmes, Ann, 47
Holt, Richard, 78
Home, Lord, 92
Howe, Sir Geoffrey, as Hearth Rug, 29; as rainmaker, 30; as playboy diplomat, 80–81; meanders, 138–139
Hughes, Simon, 55
Hurd, Douglas, at Conservative Women's Conference, 65; admonishes Hattersley, 72; barks, 118; bores, 123

I

Ingham, Bernard, 124–126

J

Jackson, Rev Jesse, 88–90
Jacobs, David, 15
Jarvis, Fred, 52–53
Jenkins, Lord, 25–26, 112
Jessel, Toby, 11, 68
Johnston, Sir Russell, 139
Jordan, Bill, 52–53
Joseph, Sir Keith, 92

K

Kaufman, Gerald, 101, 138
Kellett-Bowman, Dame Elaine, screeches, 13; shrills, 152
Kennedy, Charles, 56, 109, 112
Kent, Clark, 82
King, Dr. Martin Luther, 55, 90
King, Tom, 85, 100, 148

K

Kinnock, Glenys, 61–62
Kinnock, Neil, similarity to Kenny Rogers, 14; and to Basil Fawlty, 14, 38–39; at conference, 37–8, 60–61; as Mrs T's son, 40–42; similarity to General Tom Thumb, 42–43; and Ron Brown, 44–45; yobspeak of, 47–48; as Bogart, 49; in luxury hotel, 58–59; meets babies, 61–62; 70, 123, full of beans, 131; shuts up Dalyell, 140; titters at Heath, 146; humiliates Denzil Davies, 157; giggles like baby, 157
Kissinger, Dr Henry, SEE Beith, Alan
Knight, Dame Jill, bouncy, 46
Kray, Reginald, 92

L

Lane, Lois, 82
Lawson, Nigel, praised by Mrs T, 40; praised by Norman Tebbit, 42; avoided by Mrs T, 43
Lear, King, SEE Rees, Merlyn
Livingstone, Ken, on civil war, 61; covered in paint, 62; at Conservative Women's Conference, 65; skulks, 141; names names, 153–154
Longford, Lord, 96–97
Luce, Richard, 76–77, 79, 125, 150

M

Major, John, 134, 142–143
Margaret, HRH Princess, 92
Marlow, Anthony, 142
Martin, John, 112
Mayhew, Lord, 95
Meacher, Michael, as Mr Average, 75; boring, 78; parentage, 156
Meadowcroft, Michael, 55
Mellish, Lord, 96
Miles, Michael, SEE Young, Lord
Mitchell, David, 71
Mitterand, President, 95
Molyneaux, James, 119
Mona Lisa, SEE Maclennan, Robert
Moore, John, Kinnock on, 47; croaks, 48; yodels, 63–64; flirts, 65–66; elocutes, 80; fails, 134–135; fails again, 135–136
Morecambe, Eric, 81
Morgan, Rhodri, 127
Moynihan, Colin, 86
Murray, Len, 92, 95

Mac

Mac, Uncle SEE Paisley, Ian
Mackay, Andrew, 142
Maclennan, Robert, as defrocked Viscount, 54–55; 56, as Mr Maclaren, 76; as Reperata, 102–103; neat hair, 104; uncanny similarity to ventriloquist's dummy, 107; purpose of, 109; as Mona Lisa, 112; poor Bob, 141–142; rises, 154; 155, 156, 174, 175
McNamara, Kevin, 85
McTell, Ralph, 26

N

Nellist, Dave, bearded, 13; hairy, 75; fails to irritate, 131–132; leaps to feet, 156
Newton, Tony, 134
Noakes, John, 123

O

Owen, Dr David, 'fatuous impudence' of, 29; murdered, 55–57; and David Steel, 100–101; and Robert Maclennan, 102–103; excluded, 103; embarks on great adventure, 106; as 'insignificant splinter', 109; in by-election, 112–113; as 'irrelevancy', 114; and Tebbit, 134; the four faces of, 149–150